A Heart in Politics

Jeannette Rankin

and

Patsy T. Mink

D1558641

SUE DAVIDSON

SEAL PRESS

Book and cover design by Clare Conrad

Library of Congress Cataloging-in-Publication Data

Davidson, Sue, 1925–
A Heart in Politics : Jeannette Rankin and Patsy T. Mink
(Women Who Dared Series)
1. Women legislators—United States—Biography.   2. Women in politics—United States—History—20th century.   3. Rankin, Jeannette.   4. Mink, Patsy T., 1927–   .   5. United States—Congress—Biography.   6. United States—Politics and government—20th century.   I. Title.   II. Series.
E747.D28   1994   328.73'092'2—dc20 [B]   94-11066
ISBN 1-878067-53-2

First printing, October 1994
10 9 8 7 6 5 4 3 2 1

Distributed to the trade by Publishers Group West
Foreign distribution:
In Canada: Publishers Group West Canada, Toronto, Ontario
In the U.K. and Europe: Airlift Book Company, London

Acknowledgments:
All photos of Jeannette Rankin are reprinted by permission of the Montana Historical Society, except for page 6, reprinted by permission of The Bettman Archive.
All photos of Patsy T. Mink are reprinted courtesy of Patsy T. Mink, except for the cover photo (also appears on page 100), reprinted by permission of The Bettman Archive.

To Horty

For a strength that endures
and a funny bone
that won't be broken

Author's Acknowledgments

In the course of gathering material for this book and putting it into its final form, I have had help from a number of sources.

I am much indebted to the critical comments of those who read the manuscript in draft. My special thanks to Lora Myers and Joan Behar, literacy curriculum specialists, New York, for their patient reading and their many valuable suggestions, and to Seattle reading experts Becky Bauen, former literacy coordinator of the Seattle Public Library, who carefully followed several drafts, and Sandra McNeill, director of Goodwill Literacy Adult Reading Center. Prof. Karen Blair, History Department, University of Washington, Ellensburg, was particularly alert to issues inherent in the early suffrage movement, as was feminist writer Anne Koedt to the nuances of the modern women's movement. I was fortunate in having not only much encouragement, but also advice on social and cultural history, from my daughter, Erika D. Gottfried, non-print curator of the Taimiment Institute Library/Robert F. Wagner Labor Archives, New York University. Finally: It is impossible to write about the life of a politician without encountering government at every turn. I am therefore especially indebted to my husband, Alex Gottfried, emeritus professor of political science, University of Washington, whose criticism clarified my presentation of various aspects of government and politics.

A test edition of chapters from a draft of the manuscript was submitted to students at the Literacy Action Center, Seattle, for their written evaluation. My warm thanks are due to Anne Helmholz, director of the center, for organizing the testing, as well as to all the students, faculty, and staff who participated.

I wish to thank Representative Patsy T. Mink for her generous responses to my questions, both in writing and in a personal interview. For information on current political issues in Hawaii, I am grateful for an interview with the late John Bose, of Maui, former bibliographer with the State Agricultural Project, University of Hawaii, and Chairman of the Citizens' Advisory Committee for the Community Plan for Haiku Paia; and with Rita De Silva, of Kauai, managing editor of *The Garden Isle*.

Written sources I consulted for information on the careers and lives of the two subjects of this book are too numerous for listing here. Among the unpublished sources, I gratefully acknowledge the *Jeannette Rankin Transcript*, Oral History Project, The Bancroft Library, University of California, Berkeley; and the use of materials from the transcript of an oral history interview with Patsy T. Mink, conducted by Fern S. Ingersoll for the Association of Former Members of Congress, on file at the Sophia Smith Collection, Northampton, Massachusetts. Additional basic sources were *Jeannette Rankin, First Lady in Congress: A Biography*, by Hannah Josephson; "Jeannette Rankin: Suffragist, First Woman Elected to Congress, and Pacifist," a doctoral dissertation by Ted Carlton Harris; and "Patsy Takemoto Mink: Political Woman," a doctoral dissertation by Anne Russell.

My deep appreciation goes to the excellent staff of the Seattle Public Library, who always ran that extra mile, without even puffing. And sincere thanks to my Seal Press editor, Faith Conlon, for raising appropriate questions on substance and form, thereby improving the readability of the manuscript throughout.

For any errors of fact or the interpretation of facts and events in the lives of my subjects, I take sole responsibility.

These stories contain some scenes and details which are imaginary. The basic facts and main events are a true record of the lives of Jeannette Rankin and Patsy Takemoto Mink. All quotations that appear in bold print are taken directly from interviews, articles, and other records of the subjects' lives. Most shorter quotations are also from existing records; others have been created from a background of fact.

Contents

Introduction

This book tells the stories of Jeannette Rankin and Patsy Takemoto Mink, two daring American women. They grew up many years and many miles apart. Both women wanted to make the world a better place. Both chose a path in life that has been unusual for women. They became politicians.

Both women succeeded in being elected to the United States Congress. Few women in the history of this country have been elected to Congress. In fact, very few women have even tried.

Jeannette Rankin, of Montana, was the first woman to run for Congress. She won her race. In 1917, she became the first woman in Congress. Nearly fifty years later, in 1965, Patsy T. Mink began to serve in Congress. An Asian-American from Hawaii, she was the first woman of color to win a seat in Congress.

Patsy T. Mink was serving in Congress while this book was being written. Jeannette Rankin died in 1973, twenty years earlier. For this reason, there are differences in the way the women's stories are told. You will notice that, often, Patsy tells her own story, from today's viewpoint. Jeannette's story is told looking back on a life that is past.

These days, many more women are running for public office. In 1992, called the Year of the Woman, 170 women ran for Congress. That was a record high, and a good number won.

Little by little, women are starting to change the white, male world of U.S. political power. By daring to enter that world at an earlier, harder time, Jeannette Rankin and Patsy T. Mink helped light the way for those who followed.

JEANNETTE RANKIN

The Rankin family, about 1895. Back row, left to right: father, John; Jeannette; Harriet; photo of Philena (who died in childhood); Wellington; and mother, Olive. Seated in front are Mary, Edna, and Grace.

Jeannette Rankin in 1917, just before she took her seat in Congress. She was the first woman elected to Congress, at a time when most people thought women didn't have enough sense to hold public office. Her pose in this picture is firm and business-like.

NATIONAL AMERICAN
WOMAN SUFFRAGE ASS'N

April 2, 1917, the day Jeannette Rankin was sworn into Congress. She is speaking to her supporters from the balcony of the National American Woman Suffrage Association headquarters, in Washington, D.C. Behind her is Carrie Chapman Catt, president of the suffrage association.

Jeannette Rankin, undated photo. As the only member of Congress to vote against U.S. entry into both World Wars, she showed her strength and courage. Her sense of humor also helped to keep her going.

Jeannette Rankin spent many years lobbying against war. Here she speaks to a committee of Congress, arguing against the growth of the U.S. Navy. The year was 1939, when she was nearly sixty, not long before she was elected to Congress for the second time.

CHAPTER 1

Daddy's Girl, Mother's Boy

Sometimes Jeannette felt sorry for her little brother, Wellington. Wellington! What a name! A name for a stuck-up crybaby. Jeannette knew that Wellington wasn't stuck-up or a crybaby. He had been named for a friend of the family, a Dr. Wellington. His name wasn't Wellington's fault, thought Jeannette.

She held her brother down in the dirt, one knee pressed into his chest. "Come on," she said. "Give it back, thief. Now!"

"Oh, all *right!*" Wellington said. "Let me up!"

Jeannette rolled away and then stood, brushing leaves from her skirt. When Wellington stood, his dark head just reached his sister's shoulder. His hair was a darker shade of brown than hers. They both had strong black eyebrows. They looked a lot alike.

Wellington handed Jeannette a small object. It was an American Indian charm, carved out of elk horn. He had snatched it from Jeannette when she bent to pick it out of the dirt.

"I don't care," Wellington said. "It's not the last Indian carving I'll ever see."

That was true enough. Jeannette and Wellington Rankin lived in the new state of Montana. At this time, in the early 1890s, bands of Indians often passed through Missoula, Montana, the Rankins' home town. Indian people were also settled nearby. The Rankin children sometimes attended Indian tribal ceremonies with their parents.

Not many years had passed since the days of warfare between white settlers and Indian people. All their young lives, Jeannette and Wellington had heard stories about these "Indian wars."

Jeannette liked best the story told by her father, John Rankin. It was about the Nez Perce Indians and their leader, Chief Joseph. Forced off their lands by the U.S. government in 1877, the Nez Perce decided to move to Canada. In the mountains of the Montana Territory, they were stopped by soldiers and armed volunteers. "Give up your guns," demanded the captain of the white troops. "If not, we'll fight you for them."

Chief Joseph said that his people needed their guns for hunting. If not, they would starve. "We will not use our guns against you," said the chief. "We want no blood shed, white or Indian." But the captain refused to believe him. Chief Joseph asked to have one night, to think the matter over. While the white troops slept, Chief Joseph led his people upward to a high ridge. The Nez Perce then crossed the mountains, without firing a single shot.

The Nez Perce never reached Canada. Later on, they were forced to surrender to other white soldiers. Yet John Rankin told this story with great admiration for Chief Joseph. He also voiced his scorn for the captain and his troops. They were too dull, he said, to see that there were other ways of settling a question than fighting over it. Then he would add, in a dry voice: "I was one of the volunteers with the captain's troops."

Jeannette admired her father for being able to look

honestly at those "on his side"—and at himself. Like her father, she also admired Chief Joseph, a man of peace. In the future, Jeannette was to devote herself to lifelong work for world peace. The seed for that work may have been planted by her father's story of Chief Joseph.

If Jeannette admired her father, her father also admired Jeannette. She was the first child born to him and Olive (Pickering) Rankin, a pioneer school teacher. The date of Jeannette's birth was June 11, 1880. Over the next dozen years, five more girls were born, although one died in childhood.

In the middle of the girls was the fourth-born, Wellington. He was the only boy, and he was his mother's darling. Anything Wellington did was all right with her.

Meanwhile, a special bond grew between Jeannette and her father. Like him, she was endlessly curious, good with her hands, and not afraid of hard work. Like him, she was both a dreamer of dreams and a practical person.

• • •

Behind the snow-tipped mountains, the wide Montana sky was turning pink. It was getting on toward sunset. Jeannette and Wellington made their way, on horseback, across the Rankin ranch. They were heading for the road that ran between the ranch and nearby Missoula. Their father came along that road each evening after his work in town.

Jeannette sighed. "The summer's nearly over. I wish it had just begun! I wish we could live at the ranch all year around."

"Me, too," said Wellington. "But—I don't know. Maybe I'd miss Missoula, after a while. School, and everything."

"School!" Jeannette said. "*I* wouldn't miss school. Everybody repeating the same things, out of the same book. Boring!"

She held a hand across her forehead to shield her eyes from the sun. "There's Daddy. But what's wrong? He's not riding Star. He's leading him."

Hurrying their horses, the children drew near Mr. Rankin and Star. Now they could see that Star was hurt. A patch of his flesh hung down from a bleeding wound.

Mr. Rankin shouted, "Jeannette! Star ran into some barbed wire! Get needle and thread! Hot water! Meet me at the stable!"

Jeannette took off at a gallop for the ranch house. A short while later she was in the stable, bending over Star. Gently, talking to the animal the whole time, she washed the wound. She grasped her darning needle. As Mr. Rankin and Wellington watched, Jeannette sewed Star's torn flesh.

It was a neat job. John Rankin felt proud of his daughter's cool head and her skill. Still, he wasn't really surprised. He had learned to expect a lot of Jeannette.

At this time, Jeannette was twelve years old. Her life was fortunate. Her parents were kind, and lively, and bright. By the time she was born, her father had begun to make a small fortune. He had helped Missoula grow from a frontier village into a town. He had come there from Canada, in 1870, with little but his dreams of the West and his skills as a carpenter. He had stayed on to become Missoula's most important builder and a leading citizen.

Besides the ranch, where crops were raised and timber grown, the Rankins had a house in town. It was a big, fine house, the first in Missoula to have central heating. It even had a modern bathroom, with a tin bathtub.

Although the family was well-off, the Rankin children weren't spoiled. The three oldest—Jeannette, Harriet, and Wellington—had regular chores to do. As she grew older, Jeannette helped her mother look after the younger children. She learned to cook and bake. She helped to serve the ranch hands and the guests her parents entertained. In her teens, she became good at sewing, making clothes for herself and her sisters.

But she did not do only "women's work." She chopped wood, built fires, cleared brush. She knew how to care for the horses. She could do these things as well as Wellington.

Her mother fussed over Wellington, so that he often got out of doing his chores. He was "Mother's boy." Jeannette didn't mind very much. For one thing, she liked Wellington a lot, too. He was smart and strong. She liked to argue with him and wrestle with him. For another thing—although it wasn't often said—Jeannette knew that she was "Daddy's girl."

Although Jeannette was bored by school, she loved to read. She liked to turn over ideas in her mind and talk about them. Her father always listened seriously to what Jeannette had to say. He let her tag after him and listen to his conversations with men who were leaders in Missoula. They talked about what was going on in the country and about local politics. Her father seemed to take it for granted that young Jeannette could follow these talks.

Her father's early respect for her gave Jeannette a lot of self-confidence. (Later in life, when she stood alone against the whole country, she needed her self-confidence!) More than once, she heard her father tell her mother, "Jeannette will do something important with her life." Olive Rankin agreed. "Jeannette's not just average," Olive said.

As for Jeannette, she hoped that she would at least find something *interesting* to do. But what? She thought her father's business was interesting. But in the 1890s, women did not go into business as carpenters or builders. For a while, she dreamed of being a nurse, helping people in pain as she sometimes helped animals.

So far as Jeannette knew, women had very few choices. They could become nurses or teachers. Or they could marry, stay at home, and have baby after baby, like Olive. Jeannette was very sure she didn't want to do *that*.

What work should she try to do, then, when she was grown? Jeannette had no answer to this question when she finished high school. She thought she might find the answer in college. The University of Montana was just opening its doors, in Missoula. Jeannette was a member of its first freshman class, in 1898. As in high school, Jeannette was liked by her teachers and popular with her school mates. She went to dances and parties, but not very often. She preferred to be with her large family and the many visitors who came to the Rankin home. By working hard, she passed all her courses. But after four years, graduating with a degree in biology, she had found no aim that excited her.

She felt full of energy—but with no place to put it. It was a maddening feeling. A kind of panic rose in her. In her diary, she wrote the following message to herself: "Go! go! go! It makes no difference where, just so you go! At the first opportunity—go!"

At the time she graduated, she had only two choices of somewhere to "go." Both seemed dreary to her. One was to marry one of several young men who had asked her. The other was to teach grade school in a tiny Montana town.

She went off to Whitehall, Montana, to teach school.

At the end of the school year, she was home again. "I'll never make a small-town school teacher," she told her father. "I never thought you would," he said. "You weren't meant for a life as narrow as that." Yet he did not suggest how she was to begin the wider life he believed she was meant for.

Not knowing what else to do, she went to work for a Missoula dressmaker. She continued to help Olive with household tasks. She was doing the same things she had done since her teens. "Go! go! go!" she thought. But she did not seem to be going anywhere.

And then, in 1904, a great shadow fell upon her life. John Rankin became ill with Rocky Mountain spotted fever, and died.

He had provided well for his wife and children. His estate was worth over $100,000. It was a lot of money for those days. Still, there were five more children who had to be supported through college. There was money enough, but it had to be spent carefully.

Wellington and Harriet were both at colleges in Montana now. By the time Mr. Rankin died, Wellington had decided to become a lawyer. Olive and John had always wanted him to have the best education possible. The family agreed that he should go East.

So on a bright autumn morning, "Mother's boy" got on board a train to Boston, Massachusetts. He was headed for Harvard University. Left behind, waving until the train could no longer be seen, was a very lonely, twenty-four-year-old "Daddy's girl."

CHAPTER 2

To Be of Use

"Please come for a visit," Wellington's letter said. "The Boston cousins want to see you, and so do I."

It didn't take Jeannette long to decide to take the trip. She wanted to meet her mother's relations in Boston. She wanted to visit Cambridge, too, home of Harvard University, near Boston. She had dreamed of traveling, but she had never been outside Montana. Within a few months of saying goodbye to Wellington, she was saying hello to him again.

Jeannette was only medium height, and slender—not easy to see in a crowd. But Wellington, in the crowd at the station, spotted her the minute she stepped from the train.

"My, you look fine, Jeannette," he said. She had not looked as well as this since before their father died. She wore a high-collared coat and a wide-brimmed hat of deep brown. The color accented her mass of shining brown hair. Her cheeks were pink with the cold and with excitement.

Brother and sister talked without stopping as they left the station. "How I've missed you, Jeannette!" Wellington said when they were seated in a cab. "There's no one here who understands me as well as you. And nobody I'd rather talk to."

The cab was moving forward through narrow streets. Jeannette had become silent. The smile on her lips, Wellington saw, had gone. With wide eyes, she was gazing through the windows. Wellington's glance followed hers.

On both sides of the street were shabby buildings with broken bricks and peeling paint. Some thin, white-faced children could be seen at the dirty windows. The snow piled up along the street was black with dirt and mixed with trash. People in ragged clothing and worn, cracked shoes, waded through the snow.

Jeannette took in a sight she'd never seen until now. It was the deep poverty of a big Eastern city. She had read about it, but it had not seemed real to her. There weren't any places like this in Montana. There was little poverty, except among Indian people. And Jeannette hadn't spent much time with Indians. She didn't know how they really lived.

It wasn't hard for Wellington to read Jeannette's thoughts. "Not much like Montana, is it?" he said quietly.

Jeannette's face had lost some of its rosy color. In a low voice, she said, "Doesn't anyone care about—about this?"

"Oh, yes," Wellington said. "Even apart from God— who certainly doesn't seem to be on the job here. But there are all sorts of reformers at work in the slums. They care."

"Which reformers? Who?"

"Oh . . . all sorts." Wellington seemed less sure of himself now. "You can find out for yourself, by reading. You can use the Harvard library. I'll fix it."

So it was that Jeannette spent most of her Eastern visit in the Harvard library. The library was quiet. But inside

Jeannette there was an uproar. New facts and ideas were crowding her brain. She was learning what the reformers were doing, to try to improve the lives of the poor.

They were fighting to make cities collect garbage in run-down neighborhoods. They were struggling to bring health care to the people there. They were getting libraries to open branches in these areas. They were teaching English to immigrants and sending poor children to summer camps. They were fighting for safer working conditions in places where poor people worked.

Much of this reform work was carried on through neighborhood centers, called "settlement houses." Jeannette learned about the first and most famous of these. It was called Hull House, in Chicago. It had been started in 1889 by a woman, Jane Addams. Many other reform leaders and workers were women. A lot of them had started as social workers at Hull House.

Reading, Jeannette felt as though she were waking up from a long sleep. "All this time," she thought. "All this time, I might have been of *use* to people!"

By the time she went back to Missoula, she knew what she wanted to do. She wanted to join the reform movement.

But in Missoula, there was no movement to join. After a time, she went to San Francisco. There, she worked directly with the poor, in a settlement house. She made up her mind to follow a career as a social worker.

In the autumn of 1908, Jeannette left for New York. She entered the New York School of Philanthropy, a leading social work school. She did well in her courses. More important, she came in contact with many outstanding reformers. They were exciting people, with a passion to make society better. She carried the excitement with her, to her first social work job. It was in a home for orphans, in Spokane, Washington.

Her excitement soon turned to heartache. Discipline was strict at the orphan home—as if it were a jail. The children were treated coldly. It was nearly impossible to find families that would adopt them. Jeannette never forgot a miserable scene that took place before her eyes. "One child was placed in a home and they decided they didn't want him. He came back and wept in the office."

Jeannette thought: "I can't bear this." But as a newcomer, she had no power to change anything. Each time she was kind to a child, she was told she had broken some rule.

Unable to help the children, even in small ways, she quit the job. She hated herself for this. "I have failed these children!" she thought. "I am a failure. I'm going *nowhere!*"

But Jeannette was wrong. She was getting closer to finding her path in life. She didn't know this. She knew only that she felt deeply ashamed. Too ashamed to go back to Missoula. She wrote to her family. She said that she had decided to attend the University of Washington, in Seattle. Although the term didn't start for two months, she packed and left.

On the train, the faces of the unloved orphans swam before her. Tears came to her eyes. She dabbed at them with her handkerchief. "Now, then," she said to herself, "crying isn't going to help those children." But what would help them? she thought. Certainly, in this case, social work wasn't the answer.

She sighed and picked up the newspaper she'd bought

in Spokane. She'd been too wrapped up in her job to notice the newspapers lately. As she read now, her eyes grew alert.

In the paper was a letter from a suffragist. She was one of a number of people who were working for women's right to vote. Women's groups had been working for this right for more than fifty years. But the men who held power in the country feared giving women the right to vote. They thought that women would use it to overturn everything—especially to make the rich and the poor more equal. And many men—those who held power and those who didn't—thought women hadn't the sense to vote wisely.

In the whole United States, then, only four states had so far given women voting rights. They were all Western states—Wyoming, Utah, Colorado, and Idaho. Now, in 1910, there was to be a vote on woman suffrage, in another Western state. That state was Washington. Since Jeannette was living in Washington, for the moment, she read the letter in the newspaper with care.

Clearly, the woman who wrote the letter *did* want to make the rich and poor more equal. Until women got the vote, she wrote, they had no influence on laws. And better laws were needed to improve the working and living conditions of the poor. That was why poor and working-class women—who must earn their own bread—needed the vote, stated the letter. The letter-writer did not believe that "rich, educated women have suffered enough" to care deeply.

Now Jeannette's cheeks burned. She felt that the letter-writer was speaking about her. "But I do care—I do!" she thought. "And haven't I been trying—trying to be of use? Trying in every way I know?" Yes. But perhaps there were some ways she hadn't thought about.

She decided that she would begin to think of them now.

• • •

In Seattle, Jeannette rented a small room in a tree-shaded house near the university. Soon after she was settled, she found her way to the office of the Washington Equal Suffrage Association.

It was noon. A number of women were at a table, eating lunch. They were deep in conversation. One of them looked up and said, "Oh, hello, you must be Miss Roe!" She nodded toward another table. "The posters are over there. Please put up a lot, if you can. It's not a popular job, so far. And thanks!"

The heading on the posters read, "Votes for Women!" Jeannette didn't want to interrupt the women. So she didn't say that she was not Miss Roe. She picked up a pile of posters and went out again. In a little over an hour, she returned.

Jeannette was reaching for another pile of posters, when one of the women said, "Miss Roe! You've put up all those posters?"

Jeannette nodded. Another of the women said: "Where?"

"Well, all around," said Jeannette. "Fences, tree trunks, store windows. The barbershop—"

"The barbershop! That male kingdom!" It was a tall, pretty woman, with dimples, who said this. "How did you do that?"

"I just walked in and asked," said Jeannette. "As I did in the other stores. Nicely, of course. I told the owner it was only fair that men should vote for women's right to vote. If men don't vote for our rights, I said, *we'll* never get a chance to vote, at all."

A small, dark woman said, "You are a wonder, Miss Roe!"

Jeannette hadn't smiled much lately. She smiled now.

"I'm not Miss Roe," she said. She held out her hand. "My name is Jeannette Rankin."

Beginning with that day, Jeannette was swept up in the Washington campaign for woman suffrage. It was her first political experience. She learned fast, from smart, capable women leaders. She learned how to organize for an election. She learned how to find campaign supporters, how to put them to work, how to keep track of what they did. She learned how to reach the voting public—all men —and what to say about suffrage.

All the while, her mind was buzzing. She felt she'd found the key to the problems of human misery that had troubled her. The key was better laws, she thought, to bring about better conditions. But half the adults in the country—the female half—had little to say about laws. Until women got the vote, they could have no direct influence on the laws that ruled their lives, their children's lives, and the life of the whole nation.

So thinking, Jeannette worked harder than ever on the campaign. When election day came, in November, there was a great victory. Suffrage was voted in, by nearly two-to-one. The women—Jeannette only one among thousands of them—had done their work well.

Yet, as Jeannette returned home for the Christmas holidays, she knew that more work lay ahead. In forty-two states, women still had no vote.

In fact, her own state, Montana, was one of them. But a few days after Jeannette got home, she learned something interesting. A bill calling for a public vote on woman suffrage was soon to be brought before the Montana legislature.

Jeannette made a sudden, bold decision. She wrote and asked if she might speak to the legislature in favor of the bill. Her request was quickly granted—somewhat to her surprise. Probably, it was because her father's name was known in Montana. She was invited to speak before the state House of Representatives on February first.

It wasn't the first time such bills had come before the legislature. They had been proposed before, in recent years, and each time turned down. Most of the lawmakers saw them as a joke.

Something was new, this time, however. No woman had ever made a speech to the Montana legislature. The event was historic, a break-through for women.

Still, Jeannette didn't feel very nervous. She had taken a class in public speaking at the University of Washington. She'd made a few speeches to small groups, in Seattle, which had gone pretty well. It was Wellington who was nervous. During the holidays, he helped Jeannette rewrite her speech. "Now memorize it," he said. Jeannette rehearsed the speech before him, over and over.

"You must have a new dress," said Wellington. "Blue, I think. You look marvelous in blue. Blue velvet, under lace."

"Oh, Wellington...no." Jeannette was thinking of the newspaper letter about "rich women." "It will cost too much."

"Nonsense. It's important for you to look your best."

A great many people wanted to hear a woman speak before the legislature. On February 1, 1911, the House was jammed. The lawmakers had decked the room with flowers. They had also removed the spittoons and had voted to forbid cigars. That was because of the many women who were attending, for the first time.

Into this male kingdom Jeannette Rankin stepped. Her opening words, spoken in a ringing voice, were: "I was born in Montana." These simple words brought instant, wild applause. Few people living in the far Western state of Montana had been born there. Now Jeannette continued, speaking with force. She reminded the lawmakers of women's part in Montana's history. Since pioneer days, women had worked on farms and the range, in homes and schools. Men had welcomed their help. How much longer, then, would men deny them their fair share in self-government?

Jeannette reminded the legislators that women paid taxes. "At the beginning of this country's history," said Jeannette, "men gave their lives for a principle. It was: Taxation without representation is tyranny! Women struggle now for the same principle: 'No taxation without representation!'"

Finally, Jeannette pointed out that in the most advanced countries of the world, women voted. She reminded the lawmakers that Montana's neighbor states— Wyoming, Colorado, Utah, and Idaho—had granted suffrage to women. "Where will Montana stand?" asked Jeannette. Looking around the chamber at the legislators, she ended: "Gentlemen, where will *you* stand?"

The applause now was loud and long. Members of the legislature shook her hand. Suffragists crowded around to thank her. Reporters moved in to ask questions. Camera lights flashed.

Jeannette's speech received much publicity. There were many articles about her in the newspapers. Jeannette

Rankin's name became known throughout Montana.

And soon it became clear that a lot of lawmakers had taken her speech to heart. While the suffrage bill didn't pass, the vote was very close. With this good start, hopes were high for future success.

Jeannette was elated. First in Washington, now in her home state, she had brought real help to the suffrage cause. Where all this was leading, she still didn't know. She only knew that, at last, she had begun to feel of use.

CHAPTER 3

Traveling the Country
for the Vote

A lot of eyes were on Jeannette now—not only in Montana. National leaders of the suffrage cause had begun to notice her. It wasn't long before an exciting offer came to her. She was asked to take a job with the New York Woman Suffrage Party. By May of 1911, she was on her way to New York City.

For years the struggle for women's right to vote had been in a slump. So far, the women had failed to get the all-male Congress to support a woman suffrage amendment to the U.S. Constitution. They had not given up that attempt, which was the path to making woman suffrage the law of the land. Meanwhile, they had also been working to gain the right to vote in various states. The victory in Washington State, where Jeannette had worked, was therefore very important. It was the first state to grant women voting rights in fourteen years.

One of Jeannette's first tasks in her new job was to hold street corner meetings. It was hard to attract busy New Yorkers. But she learned a way. When she saw anyone friendly-looking, she would ask: "Can you stay for a few moments?" Soon, more people would halt. Then one of the suffragists would climb up on a box to speak, while others gave out leaflets to the crowd.

Another task was getting people to sign petitions. These were statements in favor of a state suffrage law. Jeannette took these wherever people gathered. She wasn't too shy to go alone into bars and cafes to speak to people. Her air of cheerful confidence was the same, no matter where she went. The reason was simple: she believed in what she was doing. So why be shy?

As during her last New York stay, Jeannette met many interesting people. She was drawn into a circle of talented, high-spirited women. They included artists, writers, teachers. Among them was Katherine Anthony, who was soon to make her mark as an author. She and Jeannette formed a special friendship, which became life-long.

A small group of these women, calling itself the Dinner Club, met once a week. These friends of Jeannette weren't simply suffragists, they were feminists. Their interests went far beyond voting rights for women. They wanted equality in education, in jobs and salaries. They wanted daycare centers for working mothers. They wanted women to have access to birth control and abortion. Many of the dreams of the Dinner Club members came to pass. Even so, none of the rights they discussed and worked for is secure today.

Jeannette did not stay put in New York for very long. She was "loaned" to the suffrage campaign in California. When the suffrage amendment had passed there, she went back to New York. At the end of 1912, she took a new job. She became field secretary for the National American Woman Suffrage Association, or NAWSA. In her new job, she traveled throughout the country to advance the suffrage cause. She did this work in many ways. She gave speeches in cities and small towns. She spoke to workers in factories and on farms. She organized suffrage clubs.

She also lobbied for suffrage. That is, she talked with lawmakers, trying to get them to support votes for women. She went from state to state, to lobby the lawmakers in state legislatures. She went to Washington, D.C., to lobby the U.S. Congressmen who made laws for the whole country.

She grew more and more skilled at political work. Her open, friendly personality was a help. People inside and outside suffrage groups agreed that Miss Rankin had "great charm." Outsiders were impressed that she seemed so "feminine." (Their notion of a suffragist was someone rough and rude.)

The suffrage movement was growing stronger. Still, progress in the individual states was slow. In late 1912, the suffragists began to turn fresh attention to the hope of an amendment to the U.S. Constitution. This was in part because a new President, Woodrow Wilson, had just been elected.

The new President was going to take office in March 1913. Great crowds would gather in Washington, D.C., for the inauguration. It seemed the perfect time to hold a huge suffrage parade. A parade would make a dramatic appeal to the President, the Congress, and the crowds.

On March 3, the day before the inauguration, five thousand women came to Washington, D.C., to march. Leading the parade was a dashing white-clad woman on horseback. Behind her marched women from every state and territory. Jeannette marched at the head of the Montana group with her sister Edna. There were banners, floats, and an all-women band. In those days, before TV, parades were an important form of entertainment. And this parade had been highly publicized. An enormous crowd gathered to watch.

The march had barely started when the crowd turned nasty. Men pressed in from both sides of the street, shouting insults. They spit on the women, tripped them, pelted them with burning cigars. They slapped and hit them. Meanwhile, the police stood by, offering no help. Most shared the viewpoint of the rowdies. At last, the army was called in. Only then did the disorder end.

This shameful event had its good side. The publicity for suffrage was far greater than if the event had been peaceful. The women's conduct, too, was much admired. They had not shown fear, and they had not lost their tempers.

The riot actually showed that the women's cause was gaining ground. In the past, those who opposed suffrage had been content to make fun of it. Joking was a way of showing how unimportant the women's message was. But, by now, the suffrage movement had reached hundreds of thousands of people. Its message—that women ought to have a say about what went on in the world—didn't seem so strange any more. The opponents of suffrage, believing that a woman's home should be her whole world, were very upset. Laughter gave way to anger.

Jeannette went on traveling the country until the beginning of 1914. In that year, the people of Montana at last were going to vote on a state suffrage law. This was the event Jeannette had dreamed of.

She went home to work on the campaign.

• • •

Montana is a huge state, full of rugged mountains.

There were few cities of any size. It wasn't easy to reach the people scattered around the state. Jeannette traveled tirelessly, by train, by car, and sometimes on horseback. During one period, she covered 1300 miles in twenty-five days, giving twenty-six speeches. She spoke from courthouse steps, in country stores, in mining camps, in union halls, and in schools.

Jeannette wasn't working alone. On earlier trips home, she had enlisted women to start suffrage clubs all over the state. The people in these groups now went into action. To get out their message, they held picnics, rallies, and barn dances. They sent out thousands of pieces of mail. Well-known national suffrage leaders also helped, visiting Montana as speakers.

Jeannette's family pitched in. Her sisters worked at the main office and went door-to-door with suffrage leaflets. Wellington was president of a group called the Men's League for Woman Suffrage. To kick off the campaign, the group held a big public meeting. It took place in Helena, Montana, where Wellington, now a lawyer, had opened an office.

On the whole, the campaign seemed to go well. Still, it had some powerful enemies. People in the liquor trade didn't want women to vote. They were afraid that women would pass laws against the sale of liquor. The owners of the copper mines were also against woman suffrage. They, too, feared laws favored by many women. These were laws to improve safety in the mines, and worker compensation laws.

These big business enemies had plenty of money to use against the suffrage campaign. They had influence on Montana newspapers, most of them owned by the mining companies. They had many rich friends—some of them women—who feared change in "our way of life." Besides this, the copper mines employed a lot of men. These men knew how their bosses wanted them to vote. Some feared they might be fired if woman suffrage won.

Jeannette was aware of the forces working against the cause. But the Montana suffrage movement had strengths of its own. An early campaign letter stated: "Women in our organization are from all walks of life, every political party and every religion and faith." It was true. Therefore, the campaign appealed to many different kinds of women and men—from working-class to those in high places. Jeannette remained hopeful and cheerful.

Then, in August 1914, a blow fell upon her. She learned that war had begun between the nations of Europe. The news came like a bolt out of the blue. She had argued that women could use their voting power to prevent wars. Now a war had started—and she hadn't even seen it coming. It had crept up while her mind was only on suffrage. She was horrified. Years later, she remembered, "I felt the end of the world was coming if we were stupid enough to go to war."

Speaking to a crowd, she said, "If they are going to have war, they ought to take the old men and leave the young men to carry on the race." A newspaper sneered that such talk wasn't nice from an "unmarried woman."

Jeannette wasn't worrying about what was nice. She was struggling to overcome her hopeless feelings. As the first shock faded, she got hold of herself. At least, she thought, the U.S. wasn't in the war—yet. She could still work to prevent that.

There is a saying among the religious group called Quakers, that "it is better to light a candle than to curse the darkness." This saying fit the way Jeannette lived her life. Her answer to despair was action.

Many Montana suffragists agreed with Jeannette's views on war. An anti-war message was now heard much more often in the suffrage campaign. Jeannette recalled:

In talking to women, urging suffrage, we said over and over again that war was stupid and couldn't be used successfully to change human relationships. . . . It was women's work which was destroyed by war. Their work was raising human beings, and war destroyed humans to protect profits and property.

Montana's business leaders feared that *their* "profits and property" were in danger, if women got the vote. They were willing to go very far to prevent this. Jeannette knew they might even try to steal the election. This had happened in some other states. Workers at voting places had been bribed by powerful enemies of suffrage, to make changes in the ballots. Jeannette made up her mind not to let that happen in Montana.

On Election Day, women's groups watched the most important voting places. Local lawyers oversaw the count. These measures to prevent fraud were taken under Jeannette's direction.

Then began a long wait for the election results. While the ballots were being counted, Jeannette was expected in Nashville, Tennessee. The National American Woman Suffrage Association was holding its yearly convention there. Jeannette sent a telegram to the convention. She said that she would not attend unless the Montana suffrage measure passed.

At last, in mid-November, the tally was complete. By a vote of 41,301 to 37,588, the suffrage measure won.

Jeannette threw some belongings into a suitcase. The

happy news about Montana ran ahead of her to Nashville. When she stood before the meeting, the women burst into wild applause. They knew that she had struggled for the vote all around the country. They also understood how much Montana meant to her.

It meant a lot to them, as well. It was the tenth state that had granted women the vote. Nevada had recently become the ninth. True, neither of these states had many people. Their political importance was not great. What was important was the proof that the cause had strong, effective workers on its side.

While she was in Nashville, Jeannette found the energy to address a street meeting. She also dropped in at Vanderbilt College. After she spoke to students there, she was able to start a suffrage group, with forty-six members.

Even so, she felt drained and tired. It wasn't so much from her endless activity. At thirty-four, she was strong and in perfect health. The strain she felt had little to do with her body.

"The war!" she thought, again and again. "The insane, unthinkable war!"

CHAPTER 4

"The Lady from Montana"

"Other people take vacations, Jeannette," Wellington said. "Why not you?"

"That's not strictly true," said Jeannette. "Lots of people without money can't take vacations."

"Good heavens, Jeannette. I've enough money to send you anywhere!" That was true. Wellington was becoming a rich man.

"I can't *go* just anywhere. There's a war on, you know."

Jeannette's sister Harriet laughed. "How stubborn you are, Jeannette! You've worked so hard. Take some time off!"

"Well," Jeannette said. "I'll think about it. I have other things to see to, first."

At this time, Jeannette had joined others who were working toward peace in Europe. Among the leaders of this effort was her early hero, Jane Addams of Hull House. Along with Miss Addams and other women, Jeannette helped to found a group called the Women's Peace Party. She helped to write peace proposals sent to leaders of the warring nations. Meanwhile, she went on with her speaking tours for suffrage. But, at last, she knew a break would be welcome. She agreed to get away awhile.

In the summer of 1915, Jeannette sailed for New Zealand. She was curious about this faraway country. Women there had won the right to vote in 1893. She wondered if they had used that power to improve laws and social conditions. Another reason she chose New Zealand was that its language was English. That would make it easier to find some sort of work, she thought. She did not want Wellington to pay for her keep.

Once settled in New Zealand, Jeannette decided to try to earn money by sewing. It was a way, she thought, to meet women in their homes. She'd be able to talk with them about how they used their voting rights. She could study their lives.

She soon had plenty of work. The New Zealand women thought that clothes made by an American were sure to be very stylish. Years later Jeannette said, with an impish smile: "By then, I had forgotten what I once knew about sewing. If I made a mistake, I'd say, 'Oh, this is the way we do it in America.'"

Jeannette lived in a cooperative home called the "Girls' Friendly." Other sewing women lived there, too. Jeannette was shocked at their low pay. She demanded twice as much for herself—and got it, too. At her urging, the other women followed her example. Their pay improved. Even far from home, Jeannette stirred things up!

She returned to the U.S. after nearly a year, in the spring of 1916. She felt rested and well. Her mind buzzed with thoughts and plans. As her ship cut through the ocean, a daring idea took hold of her. It was that she should run for the Congress of the United States.

No woman in history had ever run for Congress. But—suppose she won! What better way, she thought, to show that women could govern as well as men? What better hope of extending the vote to every woman in the country? For, with a woman in Congress to push for it, the suffrage amendment had a real chance of passing.

When she got back to Missoula, Jeannette called a meeting. Women leaders came from all over the state. They came to make political plans for the future. It was more than a year since women's voting rights had been won in Montana. The next step, the women believed, was to elect a woman to public office. They wanted Jeannette to run for public office. Because of her suffrage work, she was the best-known woman in the state.

But few agreed that she should start by running for Congress. They wanted her to start with a less important office. It didn't seem right to them, somehow, for a woman to aim so high, so fast. It seemed so pushy. Voices called out: "Why not run for the state legislature?" "Congress *later*, Jeannette!"

The next day, Jeannette had a talk with Wellington. Wellington had asked for opinions from friends who were active in state politics. None of these men thought Jeannette should run. One man said: "Don't let your sister make a fool of herself."

But unlike these men, Jeannette had made speeches on street corners. She had stopped strangers to give them leaflets. She had gone door-to-door with petitions for a cause that people often laughed at. She wasn't afraid of looking like a fool. If she had been, she would have given up her struggle long ago.

So she asked: "And what do you think, Wellington?"

Wellington grinned. "You're the best campaigner I ever saw. You'll win! I'll stake my money on it. My time, too. I'll manage your campaign, if you want me."

Sister and brother shook hands.

A month later, Jeannette Rankin announced that she was a candidate for Congress. The date was July 11, 1916.

• • •

Jeannette ran for a seat in the House of Representatives as a Republican. Her family was Republican, and she didn't see any reason to change to a different party. Party labels didn't mean much to Jeannette, anyway. In an interview many years later she said: "I never was a Republican. I ran on the Republican ticket."

To most women in Montana, Jeannette's party label didn't matter, either. As soon as they heard that she was a candidate, they flocked to help her campaign. There were Democrats among them as well as Republicans. There were Socialists and members of various small political parties. They could all see that electing a woman to Congress would give woman suffrage a big boost.

The women who had urged Jeannette not to run for Congress changed their minds. Seeing others behind Jeannette, they joined her, too. They felt a little ashamed of their earlier doubts.

Jeannette's sisters, Harriet, Grace, Mary, and Edna, quickly took up campaign tasks. Edna, the youngest, pitched in, although she was in law school. It was rare for a woman to go to law school in those days, but the Rankin sisters were unusual. (Harriett and Mary also had careers, later in life. Harriett became Dean of Women at the University of Montana, and Mary taught English there.) At the time of Jeannette's campaign, the older sisters were married, and two had small children. But every member of her family, starting with her mother, found time for Jeannette's campaign.

The suffrage clubs of Montana hadn't melted away

after their victory in 1914. They had re-formed as Good Government Clubs. These clubs now became the base for Jeannette's campaign. Their members went to work for her all over the state.

The first contest she had to win was the Republican primary election. Besides Jeannette, seven men were in this race. The two highest winners would face two Democrats in November.

Rankin workers were still busy the day of the primary. They called everyone who had a telephone. "Good morning! Have you voted for Jeannette Rankin?" their cheery voices asked. When the votes had been counted, Wellington's political friends were in for a surprise. Jeannette got the highest vote of all eight candidates. She led her closest rival by more than 7000.

These results made the other candidates sit up and take notice. Until now, they hadn't taken Jeannette seriously. Now they began to listen to what she was saying.

What she said was clear. First, she called for amending the Constitution to give women the vote nationwide. Next, she pledged to work for the interests of children. The previous Congress, she said, had earmarked $300,000 for a study of hog feed. It had set aside only $30,000 to study children's needs. "If the hogs of the nation are ten times more important than the children, it is high time that women should make their influence felt," she said. Finally, she promised to do all in her power to keep the country out of war. No promise was nearer her heart.

Jeannette's campaign wasn't like that of the other candidates. Their way was to give a prepared speech, in a public hall. Unlike them, Jeannette continued to speak on street corners, in kitchens, in mines and lumber camps. She drove her car over bumpy roads to reach wheat farmers and sheep herders. Her opponents, she said, had "too much dignity" to go out and meet people this way.

Her popularity grew. When she did talk at indoor meetings, they were packed. Often people had to be turned away, or stand to hear her. She was a powerful speaker. She made her listeners clap, laugh, stomp their feet. They cheered, "Rankin, Rankin!"

With those cheers ringing in her ears, Jeannette herself voted, November 6, 1916. She felt there was something to cheer about, whether she won or lost. For one thing, for the first time in her life she could vote, because in Montana women had won that right. Furthermore, she could vote for a woman (herself!) for the U.S. Congress. It was a choice voters never had before.

Jeannette went home, where she and her mother passed a restless day. In those days, the votes were counted by hand. It took a long time to get election results. At one o'clock the next morning, Jeannette couldn't bear the waiting. She telephoned a Missoula newspaper to learn what the count was, so far. She didn't want to reveal who she was. So she asked: "How did President Wilson do?" Then she asked about Jeannette Rankin.

"Oh, she lost," said the voice at the other end of the wire.

Feeling letdown and weary, Jeannette went to bed.

The next day, Wellington telephoned from Helena. He'd been studying the returns, he said, and he was sure Jeannette had won. It was another day before complete returns showed he was right.

Even then, the Missoula newspapers didn't admit that she had won. The papers were ruled by Jeannette's old enemies, the owners of Montana's mines. They didn't like her positions for a shorter, eight-hour workday and other worker benefits. They had clashed with Wellington, too. He had fought many battles against them in the courts. Yet they hadn't thought his sister much of a threat. A woman in the U.S. Congress! The idea seemed impossible to them. The papers they controlled took little notice of her campaign.

It was the same with major newspapers in other parts of the country. In New York and Washington, D.C., hardly a word about the Montana contest was printed. The *New York Times*' motto then, as now, was "All the news that's fit to print." All through Jeannette's campaign, it saw nothing fit to print about her.

Her victory therefore burst like a bombshell upon the country, and the world. After all, she wasn't just the first woman elected to the U.S. Congress. She was the first woman elected to any national governing body in the whole world.

How had she done it? Where had she got the nerve to try it? Was she pretty? Was she married? Did she have a sweetheart? Reporters poured into Missoula for answers to such questions.

"The Lady from Montana," as she began to be called, was in the public spotlight now. Anything she said or did could have an effect on women's political future. Beyond that, she had a new responsibility to the people of Montana and the whole country.

She felt just a little bit scared.

CHAPTER 5

A Decision for Life

Most people didn't know what to expect of the first woman elected to Congress. Some thought that she would be heavy and mannish, with a deep voice. Others pictured a dainty girl, very young. (Jeannette was thirty-seven.) Some looked forward to a pistol-packing cowgirl, straight out of Montana's Wild West.

Since there was no TV and no radio, people got many of their opinions from newspapers. Some news writers attacked Jeannette, although they hadn't met her. They laughed at the idea that a woman could be trusted in a high position. They were sure Jeannette would soon make a fool of herself.

In fact, Jeannette was better trained for her new job than many new Congressmen. She had learned a lot working for woman suffrage laws in many states. She knew how bills were brought before legislative bodies. She knew about the rules under which laws were debated. She had spent time talking and arguing with U.S. Congressmen. She wasn't a stranger to Washington, D.C.

Jeannette made a speaking tour before taking her seat in Congress. As she set out for the tour, on February 23, 1917, she received disturbing news. President Wilson was calling for a special session of Congress, on April 2.

Everyone guessed the reason, in advance. The President was going to ask Congress to declare war on Germany.

President Wilson had been known as a man of peace. The slogan of his campaign, in 1916, was "He Kept Us Out Of War." This belief had helped to make his election a sure thing.

For when the war began, in 1914, few Americans wanted to get into the fight. On one side of that fight, at first, were Great Britain, France, and Russia. On the other side were Germany and Austria-Hungary. In time, most countries of the world joined in. Meanwhile, American businesses made a profit selling supplies to both sides. But when German submarines began sinking British supply ships, opinion turned against Germany. Americans who were passengers on those ships lost their lives. Some felt the whole United States was at risk, until Germany was defeated.

Thus the public mood began to swing toward war. The reporters following Jeannette's tour wanted to know her views. Would she vote for, or against, a war declaration? She replied, "I cannot say anything about that at this time."

It wasn't only reporters who wanted to know how Jeannette would vote. The question haunted her on every side. It was asked by those who urged her to vote yes. It was asked by those who urged her to vote no. The shadow of war darkened this time of victory in Jeannette Rankin's life.

The war darkened the victory for the suffrage movement, too. The suffragists felt that Jeannette's election was a great leap forward. They felt—and rightly—that without their work, it never would have happened. It was a glorious event, which should have brought them closer together. There were already a lot of quarrels among them. Now the war pushed them even further apart. This was because some of them were in favor of supporting a war, if it came. Others were passionately against aiding war.

But women on all sides of the quarrel came together on April 2, 1917. It was first day of the special Congressional session called by President Wilson. It was also the day on which Jeannette would be sworn into Congress. To honor her, suffrage leaders held a breakfast at a Washington, D.C. hotel.

Looking around the table, Jeannette beheld well-known faces. There was Julia Lathrop, appointed by President Taft to head the first Children's Bureau. There was the writer Katherine Anthony, a dear friend. There were the famous suffragists Carrie Chapman Catt and Alice Paul. These two were the leaders of the opposing sides. Alice Paul was a pacifist, against all wars. Carrie Catt wanted votes for women more than anything, even more than peace. She feared that if suffragists didn't back a war effort, their cause would lose respect.

Jeannette was under pressure from both women. Both believed that her vote for or against war was of the greatest importance. They knew that she would be viewed as speaking for all women. Jeannette knew it, too. The responsibility lay heavily upon her. When she rose to give her speech to the women, her voice shook.

As she spoke, her voice grew stronger. Her remarks were brief. At the end of them, her voice once again trembled.

"There will be many times when I will make mistakes," she said. "It means a great deal to me to have your encouragement and support. I promise. . . . "

But what could she promise? Her voice broke. She sat down.

Jeannette was driven to the Capitol, where the Congress would soon meet. She rode in an open car decked with flags and flowers. Behind it came a parade of cars, with women from most of the forty-eight states. At the Capitol steps, reporters pounced upon Jeannette. A crowd gathered there pressed forward to glimpse "the Lady from Montana." People in the crowd were worried about the war. The festive air of Jeannette's arrival cheered them. Many shook her hand and asked for autographs.

At twelve noon, she entered the House of Representatives. She was escorted by John Evans, Montana's other representative. On her arm, she carried flowers presented to her at the breakfast. As she went down the aisle, House members and visitors—Jeannette's family among them—stood up. Everyone burst into applause. Before she could sit down, members of the House clustered around her. Democrats and Republicans alike pushed in to shake her hand.

No member of the House of Representatives had ever entered it carrying flowers. This was a moment history had not seen before. There stood Jeannette, one woman among 434 men. She did not giggle or blush. Neither did she bluster in a hearty, male way. She shook every hand offered, smiling in a friendly, calm manner. She looked, one observer wrote, "just a sensible young woman going about her business."

Jeannette and other new members were sworn into Congress that afternoon. At night, the Senate joined the House for the main business: the President's speech calling for war on Germany. At 8:30 p.m., President Wilson strode in. Jeannette sat forward tensely. She had long dreaded what was about to happen.

So had the President. President Wilson was a man of high ideals, who believed in peace. He really had tried to avoid taking the country into war. He no longer saw that as possible. Yet he could not bear the idea that he was forsaking his ideals. If he was going to lead the country into bloody struggle, he had to believe it was for moral purposes. It had to be for values that were higher than peace.

Now the President outlined those values for the Congress. The United States, he said, must protect the rights of small nations. It must join with other free nations to protect liberty. The war must be fought, he said, to bring about a just peace. And finally, in words that were to become famous: "The world," he said, "must be made safe for democracy."

A lot of people would one day come to see those famous words as an empty promise. Jeannette saw them as false from the start. All around her, people were applauding. She felt sickened.

Two days later, the Senate passed the war resolution. The vote: 82 for, 6 against, 8 not voting. Debate now moved to the House. From then on, Jeannette was not given a moment's peace.

"Everyone except the pacifists," she later recalled, "was trying to educate me to vote for war." Especially hard to bear were the arguments of pro-war suffrage friends. They told her that her vote against war would set their cause back many years. It would make enemies of men who were friendly to suffrage. Some said it would kill all hopes of ever winning the vote for women.

Wellington, too, urged her to vote "aye" for war. He was afraid a "nay" vote would show that women, all alike, were weak. It would prove that women were too soft to be trusted with the tasks of government.

But more than this, Wellington feared a "nay" vote would end Jeannette's career in politics. "You know you won't be re-elected," he warned her. That made Jeannette furious. "I'm not interested in that!" she cried. More quietly she added, "Never for one second could I face the idea that I would send young men to die, for no other reason than to save my seat in Congress."

Wellington thought, "She is so *stubborn!*" Yet he admired her honesty. They had been arguing for days. Both were worn out. "You must vote your conscience," he said, at last.

As Jeannette went back to the House chamber, she felt very much alone. By now, the country was in a fury of flag-waving. People who were against the war were being called "unpatriotic." Wilson claimed the war was for democracy and freedom. But free speech was already being taken from Americans who were against the war. Anti-war public meetings had been banned in many cities. Mobs had attacked groups that spoke out against the war. Jeannette knew attacks on freedom would grow if war came.

She also knew that her "nay" vote wouldn't stop the war. Then why not vote "aye!" urged her pro-war friends. Jeannette promised not to decide until the second roll call for votes. She promised to listen carefully to pro-war speeches in the debate.

The House debate went on all night and into the early hours of April 6. Then the first roll call for the voting began. When the clerk called Jeannette's name, a hush fell on the chamber. Jeannette said nothing. Some members thought this meant that she was confused about House rules. A leading Republican member hurried over to her and said:

> **Little woman, you cannot afford not to vote. You represent the womanhood of the country in the American Congress. I shall not advise you how to vote, but you should vote one way or the other—as your conscience dictates.**

The "little woman" knew House rules pretty well. She knew that members could vote on the first roll call, or the second, or even not vote at all. But no matter what the rules, she knew that she must vote. She would not hide.

Yet, she was suffering. Through the long hours of debate, she often sat with head in hands. She heard many loud patriotic speeches backing the war resolution. A few representatives dared to speak against it. That brought cries of "coward! liar! traitor!" Jeannette was grateful when the Majority Leader of the House rose to say, "Let me remind the House that it takes neither moral nor physical courage to declare a war for others to fight."

These words helped her when the second roll call reached her name. Every eye was on the Representative from Montana. The chamber grew completely silent as she got to her feet.

"I want to stand by my country," she said, "but I cannot vote for war. I vote no."

There was a ripple of applause. Then there was noise and confusion. Everyone was talking at once. Reporters rushed from the room, to telephone their papers. The roll call resumed, with little doubt about the results. The House voted to declare war on Germany: 373 for, 50 against, 9 not voting.

Even in the midst of the news that the country was at

war, a lot of notice was taken of the first Congresswoman. Her vote and her behavior were widely reported. Most newspapers printed stories that said she shed tears all through the roll call. The *New York Times* described her as hysterical, as well. Yet the people who sat nearest her remember her as quiet and dry-eyed.

Jeannette recalled, "I wept for a week. When the time came to vote, it was just too awful to even weep." The endless "weeping" stories, however, served a purpose. They were meant to show that women were not stable enough to serve the public. Terrific abuse was heaped upon Jeannette for her "nay" vote. She was damned up and down as "disloyal"—and a lot worse. The fifty-five others who voted "nay"—Senators and House members —got off much more lightly.

In Montana, for the moment, Jeannette remained popular. Her mail from home, before the vote, had been a whopping 16 to 1 against the war resolution. In fact, throughout the country, many people besides pacifists were opposed to the war. Only later were their voices quieted—and never altogether.

Jeannette did not regret her act. "I felt," she said, "that the first time the first woman in Congress had a chance to say no to war, she should say it. That was what held me up."

Her decision wed her to the cause of peace. It became foremost among all her concerns. And Wellington, to some extent, was wrong about her political future. One day, she would again be elected to Congress. But more important, she would go on being a politician—for peace. Her decision was for life.

CHAPTER 6

A Woman's Place Is in the House . . . of Representatives

Jeannette didn't take time to brood over the attacks upon her for her anti-war vote. She had too much work to do.

Her office was one of the busiest of any House member. The telephone rang steadily. Huge sacks of mail arrived each day. Visitors came and went on business. Some came only to look at "the lady Congressman."

Jeannette had three people helping her in the office. There were two secretaries. There was her sister Harriet Sedman, as office manager. A widow now, Harriet had recently moved to Washington, D.C., with her two little daughters. All these—plus Jeannette's mother—shared a large apartment. Katherine Anthony, who helped Jeannette write articles, often dropped in from New York.

Thus, at home, Jeannette lived in an all-women world. In Congress, of course, she was the only woman in a world of men. She had no model to follow in this position. Yet she managed gracefully. She didn't act like a helpless female. But she didn't pretend that she knew everything, either. When she needed advice or information, she asked—politely, but without apology.

She was well liked by almost all the House members.

47

They admired her directness, her honesty, her quick sense of humor. Some knew her from the time she'd spent lobbying Congress for the suffrage movement. They felt proud to introduce her to others. Before long, Jeannette was very much at home.

There were limits, however. For example, there wasn't a women's toilet for House members' use. Jeannette and her staff trudged many stairs and hallways to reach a women's public restroom. Later—after sixty years, and 100-plus female Congress members—there was still no change. Through such "messages," women were advised that *this* club didn't want them as members.

But many women, Jeannette knew, faced problems worse than that! During her two-year term, she tried to serve women—as well as children—in many ways. Her first speech in the House called for giving women equal job opportunities and pay in war industries. She argued that trained women, as well as men, were needed in the war crisis. The House passed the measure.

It seems strange that Jeannette argued for ways to help the war effort. After all, she had opposed the war. She still did. She told the Congress, "I still believe that war is a stupid and futile way of attempting to settle international disputes."

Jeannette felt, however, that now that war had come, the U.S. should try to win it quickly. If she had been a "pure" pacifist, she would have opposed *any* help to the war effort. Years later, she did adopt a "pure" pacifist stand. But it came gradually, as she thought more and more deeply about war.

While the war raged, fought in freedom's name, Jeannette battled to protect freedom at home. Very quickly, the government moved to limit free speech in the name of "security." Jeannette fought against a bill giving the government the right to censor newspapers. It also gave the government the right to imprison those who spoke against the military draft. Although Jeannette and a few others protested strongly, Congress passed the bill.

Outside of Congress a small band of women had begun another kind of protest. On January 10, 1917, suffragists holding signs began to stand at the White House gates. They were there to urge President Wilson to help get women's voting rights added to the Constitution. The pacifist Alice Paul, a friend of Jeannette, was their leader. Rain or shine, they were there. They said not a word. Their signs spoke for them:

Mr. President, What Will You Do for Woman Suffrage?

How Long Must Women Wait for Liberty?

We the Women of America Tell You That America Is Not a Democracy. Twenty Million American Women Are Denied the Right to Vote.

Today, pickets at the White House have become a common sight. But the group led by Alice Paul was the first. The women were seen as very daring. Still, at first nobody bothered them.

But as war fever grew, the women with their "unpatriotic" signs were attacked by onlookers. Police began to make arrests—of the women, not their attackers. The suffragists were held in a foul, rat-filled prison. There, hidden from the public, they were brutally mistreated—tied up, kicked, and beaten. As a protest against their treatment, the women went on a hunger strike. Their jailers force-fed them, through tubes thrust into their throats and noses.

Jeannette, who went to visit the prisoners, was horrified. She called on Congress to investigate. Soon after, public pressure caused all the women to be set free. Many people had become angry that the pickets were being abused by mobs and police. Many were impressed by their bravery, their willingness to suffer for their beliefs.

In recent months support for woman suffrage had grown a great deal. As a result of this new support, Congress was once again ready to consider a Constitutional amendment giving women the vote. Jeannette had played a major role in getting the amendment before the House. She was therefore given the honor of being the first speaker in the House debate.

The date was January 10, 1918. It was exactly a year since the silent pickets had first stood at the White House gates. Jeannette used the pickets' theme as the climax of her speech. "Shall the same Congress that voted to make the world safe for democracy," she asked, in a voice clear and firm, "refuse to give this small measure of democracy to the women of our country?"

She wasn't sure of the answer. Everyone knew the needed two-thirds vote was going to be hard to get. It was the loyalty of five men that saved the day. Four House members came from sickbeds to keep their promises to vote for the amendment. One of them was carried on a stretcher. The fifth came from his wife's deathbed. When he had voted, he left for her funeral.

The amendment passed by one vote. It was called the Susan B. Anthony Amendment, to honor the great woman suffrage leader of that name. Like other suffragists, Jeannette felt joy—but briefly. For the amendment then went on to lose in the Senate.

But it lost by only two votes, and victory was not far off. Two years later, both House and Senate passed the amendment by large votes. By then, Jeannette, who had been the first woman to work for the amendment "from the inside," was not in office.

Meantime, she used her office to try to improve the daily lives of ordinary people. She sponsored the first mother-and-child health bill ever brought to Congress. Among other things, the bill provided for education about veneral diseases and birth control. It made Jeannette some enemies, who didn't want the government in the health care business. Some also claimed to be shocked that a "spinster" knew so much about sex matters. Jeannette laughed at such comments, but she never answered them.

Jeannette had other enemies who were a more serious threat to her career. They were Montana's mine owners. While Jeannette was in Congress, there was a terrible mine accident. More than 160 men were killed. As had happened before, the deaths came about because the mine owners hadn't obeyed safety laws. Like the workers, Jeannette now wanted the federal government to take over the mines. She fought hard for this. She took the request to the President and to Congress. But despite her skills in argument, this time she did not succeed.

The mine owners were pleased at her failure. They didn't want the government butting into their business. They'd never liked Jeannette's ideas, and now she'd gone too far. They decided to put a stop to the strong-willed Miss Rankin. When she ran for Congress again, they spared no efforts to defeat her.

Jeannette fought back. Finding that her chances for a House seat were nearly zero, she ran instead for the Senate. The newspapers, most ruled by the mine owners, savagely attacked her. The main point of their attacks was her anti-war vote. While the contest was close, Jeannette still lost the Republican primary. But she ran for the Senate anyway, on a third-party ticket.

Jeannette was still very popular. The Democrat in the race was warned of this. "You have a hard fight on your hands with Jeannette Rankin in the field," his advisers said. However, he was helped by support from the leader of the National American Woman Suffrage Association. This was Carrie Chapman Catt, whom Jeannette had displeased by her vote against the war. With Catt's help, and the backing of the mine owners, the Democratic candidate won. Jeannette came in third, after the Republican.

• • •

Jeannette wasn't happy to leave Congress. She had enjoyed the work. She also knew that she was good at it. But, as usual, she looked forward, not back. At thirty-nine, much of her life was still before her. There were still many ways "to be of use."

On November 11, 1918, World War I ended, with the U.S. on the winning side. Jeannette's term in Congress ended March 4, 1919. A month later, she was on a ship bound for Europe.

With twenty-five other U.S. women on the ship, Jeannette was on a peace mission. Women from countries that had fought each other in the war were going to meet in Zurich, Switzerland. They were to work out plans for the conditions needed to prevent future wars. They called themselves the Zurich Congress.

These women were going to meet at the same time that the official Peace Conference met near Paris, France. There, only the nations that had *won* the war were represented. Leaders of those nations were going to draw up a peace treaty. The women hoped to get some of their own ideas into the treaty.

Jeannette's peace-seeking companions, led by the famous social reformer Jane Addams, were outstanding American women. They were leaders in the suffrage struggle and in many other fields. Jeannette felt humble in this group. She listened to others and talked less than usual. Even so, an observer on the trip noted: "Jeannette Rankin is clever and attractive and people are all immensely interested in her."

Among the women Jeannette got to know in the U.S. group was Mary Church Terrell. Terrell was well known as an educator, a writer, a suffragist, and a leader of black women's groups. She and Jeannette shared a hotel room and were often together.

There were no other African-Americans in the group. There were few black women in the U.S. suffrage movement, altogether. Most white suffragists wanted to keep them out. They said it was because they were afraid of the bad opinion of white Southerners. Probably, a good many were racists themselves. In fact, Jane Addams assigned Jeannette to room with Terrell because she trusted that, to Jeannette, Terrell's skin color didn't matter. But all the U.S. women felt very proud when Mary Church Terrell addressed the Zurich Congress. She gave her speech in English, then in German, then in French, all without a flaw.

The peace treaty agreed upon by the winning nations proved even worse than the women had expected. They issued a statement protesting the harsh terms the treaty forced on the losing side. The treaty called for only the losers to disarm, only the losers to pay the costs of the war. But the losing countries had nothing; the war had ruined them. Already people in Germany, especially children, were starving in large numbers. The winning side wouldn't let food get into Germany. The women in Zurich begged the Peace Conference to lift the food blockade. The blockade would "result in the spread of hatred and lead to future wars," they said.

They wired their plea to President Woodrow Wilson. His ideas on world peace had been influenced by Jane Addams and others at the Zurich Congress. He greatly respected them. But the wire he sent them from Paris said he could not help, at this time.

Before the Zurich meetings ended, the women formed a permanent organization. They called it the Women's International League for Peace and Freedom (WILPF). It was to grow far beyond the nineteen countries represented at the 1919 meeting. The oldest of present-day peace groups, it is still at work.

Jane Addams was elected WILPF's international president. Lida Heymann, a German pacifist, was chosen for international vice-president. By choosing an American and a German, the women showed their ongoing resolve to rise above the hatreds of war.

At this founding meeting in Zurich, Jeannette was elected an officer of WILPF, too. When she returned to the U.S., she went to Washington, D.C., for WILPF. Her mission was to plead with the U.S. government to lift its food blockade against Germany.

So there she was, in Washington, D.C., again. For the next twenty years, she was to spend much of her time there. Long after her 1918 defeat, her step regularly sounded and her laughter chimed in the halls of Congress. She said, "I felt as if I never left."

CHAPTER 7

From Georgia, with Love

In 1926, Katherine Anthony wrote an article about Jeannette Rankin's farm, in Georgia. Jeannette, she said, was a "pioneer." She'd bought land nobody had ever farmed before.

> She purchased sixty wild acres and set about taming them. The place was not exactly a wilderness. It was, I suppose, about as wild as the Garden of Eden must have been.

But why was Jeannette Rankin, ex-member of Congress from Montana, living in Georgia?

The answer is that Montana is far away from Washington, D.C., while Georgia is not. And it was in Washington that Jeannette mostly continued to work. Not long after returning from Europe, she took up a career as a paid lobbyist. As a lobbyist, she worked to get laws passed favoring certain causes. That meant she needed to meet and talk face-to-face with lawmakers. While sometimes she lobbied state lawmakers, more often she needed to talk with members of Congress, in Washington, D.C. It took ten days to travel round-trip by train between Montana and Washington. So Jeannette began to look for a home that was closer to her work.

She did not want this home of her own to be in a city. She loved the plain, rugged life she'd known as a child, on the ranch. She found what she wanted in Georgia. It was land in the pine country ten miles outside the city of Athens.

With the help of two carpenters, Jeannette set to work to build her house. It took four days. The house was wood, with one long room and a screened porch. There was no electricity and no running water. There was an outdoor toilet. Jeannette did her cooking on a stove in a shed behind the house. Dishes were washed near the well, amid the scent of honeysuckle and pine.

Jeannette planted 200 pecan trees and 800 peach trees as crops. There were already wild grapevines, a fig tree, wild cherry, wild plum. Jeannette canned and preserved these fruits for winter. (Her many visitors—for she loved having guests—often helped.) Since she grew and picked her own vegetables, too, she spent little money. Her material life was a lot like her neighbors', who were poor farmers.

Jeannette was living as she pleased. She was free to do this partly because she didn't want a lot of *things*. Her small income took care of her needs. She was free, too, of marriage. She didn't have to agree with anyone about how she lived.

There is no doubt that Jeannette could have married. Men were drawn by her energy and sparkle. At forty-five, she was described by Katherine Anthony as "beautiful." Maybe everyone wouldn't have agreed. But her "[prematurely] snow-white locks and her soft dark eyes" were surely striking. So the question has sometimes been asked "Why did such an attractive woman never marry?"

It's possible that Jeannette had romances, or even a love life. It might have been with one man, over the years,

or with one woman. Or she might have had several lov-
ers. But since nothing is known of it, the question is still
asked: "Why did she never marry?"

Perhaps a better question, in Jeannette's case, is,
"What for?" It seems unlikely that she wanted more family. She was part of the big, lively Rankin clan. Her sisters
now all had children. The family visited back and forth.
Jeannette had a flock of adoring nieces and nephews. One
niece lived with her on the farm for years, going to the
local grade school.

Many women, in those days, married because they
had no way to make a decent living. Jeannette didn't need
to do that. She had a small inheritance that paid her $75 a
month. It wasn't a lot, although it was worth much more
then than it is now. She usually had a job, too—even if
poorly paid. However, as she said:

> **If I haven't had anything else, I've had my freedom. I
> never did a job long unless I wanted to. I was never
> idle, but I couldn't see the purpose in most jobs I
> might have gotten.**

Jeannette had known for years that she had only one
"job," one ambition. It was to make the world a better
place. She knew that there were a lot of different ways to
do that, too. By the time she was in her thirties, she had
found the best way for her. The way for her was politics.

Jeannette knew that there was more to politics than
holding public office. Changes that help the mass of
people, she often said, don't start *at the top.* If you want
real political change, you must "work from the bottom
up," said Jeannette. Thus, the first task was to educate
people about the issues. After that, people had to let public
officials know what they wanted. That could be done in

ways ranging from letter-writing to street protests. The important thing, in Jeannette's view, was to put pressure on those who held public office. Only then was there any hope of getting them to act.

Jeannette took people through all those political steps. It was a lot of work. It meant that she could not spend much time dreaming among the Georgia pines.

• • •

When Jeannette returned from Europe, she worked for the National Consumers League. She lobbied in Congress and in state legislatures. Many of her goals were the same as those she'd worked for in Congress. She argued for child labor laws, mother-and-infant health care, a minimum wage, an eight-hour workday.

She gave up her job in 1924, to help Wellington run for the U.S. Senate. When he lost—by a close vote— Jeannette settled down on her Georgia farm. But not for long.

What Jeannette wanted most was to do work for peace. She'd never believed that World War I was fought for democracy. It had been fought, she believed, to make profits for big business. It had been fought because leaders of the military wanted more power. It had not improved the lives of ordinary Americans. It had brought ruin to Europe. To prevent the same thing from happening again, a lot had to be done, thought Jeannette.

She was ready to do a lot. She began by traveling the country for the Women's International League, speaking and lobbying. Back in Georgia, she organized the Georgia Peace Society. It met in Athens, home of the University of Georgia.

Led by Jeannette, the Georgia Peace Society held several conferences on the "Cause and Cure of War." It campaigned against building a bigger U.S. Navy. Its members urged ending the Reserve Officers' Training Corps (ROTC) in schools. The ROTC wasn't education, they said. Its only purpose was to hammer military values into the minds of students.

For a while, Jeannette had a job with the Women's Peace Union. She lobbied for an amendment to the U.S. Constitution that would outlaw war. Many groups thought that wars might be stopped if nations agreed to make war a crime.

Jeannette found lawmakers in Georgia who agreed. They asked their fellow-legislators to send a message to Congress supporting the anti-war amendment. Jeannette spoke to the legislature, to urge approval. Then she took her seat beside a powerful member, Richard Russell (later a U.S. Senator).

There was loud applause. Jeannette was pleased and excited. She whispered to Russell: "Do you think they'll pass it?"

Russell smiled. "If I think they're about to," he replied, "I'll go right down and stop it."

A few minutes later, he did just that. But Jeannette wasn't discouraged. It was a "great victory," she said, that a state legislature had discussed outlawing war at all.

By this time, in 1929, popular feelings against war had grown. The post-war "boom" had gone "bust." A lot of people were without jobs. Many now felt that the recent war had been a mistake. In this climate of opinion, many new peace groups sprang up. Now Jeannette took a job with another of these. It was called the National Council for the Prevention of War (NCPW).

Jeannette stayed with NCPW nearly ten years, at a

slim salary—$150 a month. Worse, sometimes NCPW
sent less. But she was working for the love of it. She kept
up a hectic pace.

In 1932, she organized a huge project. That June, the
Democratic and Republican parties were to hold their conventions in Chicago. Jeannette conceived the idea of a
Peace March on Chicago. Its purpose was to get both political parties to adopt a peace plank. The Peace March
gathered several thousand people from around the nation.
Many were college students. Some were disabled, jobless
war veterans. Traveling in a parade of cars from Washington, D.C., they had speaking stops along the way. They
urged people to write or wire the Chicago conventions in
favor of a peace plank.

With their peace banners flying, the parades were col-
orful. As Jeannette had foreseen, they got a lot of notice in
the news. The young people were described as "sweet."
They were not attacked by police or by crowds. Both
Republicans and Democrats listened politely to their arguments for peace. All the same—neither political party
adopted a peace plank in 1932.

Peace didn't seem very important to the main political
parties that year. The most urgent political issue was the
Great Depression. The number of homeless and hungry
kept growing. By now, nearly thirteen million Americans
were out of work. People hoped the new president they
elected that autumn would help the economy. He was a
Democrat named Franklin D. Roosevelt.

Jeannette feared war might result from efforts to
"help" the economy. She often warned about ties between
war and profit-making. In 1934—under pressure from
peace groups—the U.S. Congress began to look into
those ties. It set up a committee under Senator Gerald

Nye, to investigate arms dealers.

The Nye Committee found that arms firms had worked hard to encourage World War I. They had spread war scares and false reports. They had bribed public officials. In time of war, they had sold arms to both sides. Their profits were huge.

Jeannette spoke with anger of "our American patriots who are willing to give the life of your son for their profit." To bring more publicity to the findings of the Nye Committee, she toured the country. People were shocked by what they learned. "How can we keep this from happening again?" they asked.

One answer was proposed in a bill brought before Congress. It was supposed to take the profits out of war. For various reasons, Jeannette didn't believe the bill would work. She said it was only "a rich man's scheme to fool the people."

Jeannette went before the committee that was considering the bill. She outlined some ideas of her own. Then she ended by saying that in case a war was declared:

[The government] should pay $30 a month, or whatever a soldier's wage is, to everyone, and let everyone have a tin cup and bread card and live on the same food the soldier does, beginning with the President. For members of Congress who have voted for war, let them receive not only the $30 a month but also the honor of carrying the flag in battle, so that they would feel they are doing their bit.

Members of Congress weren't too happy at Jeannette's mocking them in that way. Still, Congress had to do something about public fears that the U.S. might be dragged into another war. In 1935, Congress passed a

Neutrality Act. The act outlawed the sale or transport of war goods to any countries at war. Jeannette led peace groups in the successful fight to get this act passed.

The act, however, had to be renewed each year. By 1937, powerful forces wanted to weaken it—including President Roosevelt. Jeannette hurried from Georgia to the Capitol, to talk and argue with members of Congress.

Jeannette's tireless activity didn't always please members of Congress. Once, when she was speaking to a Congressional committee, the chairman complained of her "meddling." "Are you," he asked Jeannette sternly, "what may be called a *lobbyist*?" He acted as if he'd never seen a lobbyist before. But Jeannette knew he saw them every day.

Jeannette was wearing a bright red hat with a feather. Her smile and her voice were as cheerful as her hat.

Yes, sir, I am a professional lobbyist. I began lobbying in 1913 for woman suffrage. I lobbied in 1915, and in the early twenties I worked for the Child Labor Amendment.

At present, she said, she had a job as a peace lobbyist for NCPW. But, she added, "I would do exactly the same work on my own."

The truth was that she was doing it "on her own" more and more now. As the Depression got worse, she could never rely on the National Council to pay her. About this time, she wrote her employer:

Am living in true Georgia fashion. No money. The stores are "furnishing" me with food and gas. They say, "It's so long since we've had any money we done got used to it."

But she could not stop working. War and the threat of war were spreading—in Asia, Africa, Europe. By 1937, there were many signs the U.S. might get drawn into these conflicts. For example, the Neutrality Act had been weakened. It now gave the President the power to let U.S. ships carry any sort of goods to nations at war. This meant putting U.S. ships at risk of armed attack. Such attacks had helped get the U.S. into World War I.

Peace groups made great efforts to inform people of the dangers. They warned that helping to arm the world was not the way to peace. They called attention to such causes of war as poverty. They held meetings, parades, and silent marches.

Jeannette, like the others, worked frantically. She went from state to state. She spoke to thousands of people, both in person and on the radio. And yet. . . . The more she did, the less effective she felt. Perhaps it was because NCWP seemed not to value her work? By 1938, she got no pay at all. She wrote the NCWP chairman:

I've no doubt money is slow coming in, but if you can send me some or put me on a weekly payroll it will help a lot. It hurts my spirit to be so broke.

She lay sleepless on her bed in Georgia. She could hear every pine cone drop. "I must find another way, a better way," she thought. "But what? What, *what*?"

The following year, she found her answer.

CHAPTER 8

"Bright Star in a Dark Night"

Morning sun glinted on green leaves. Jeannette deeply breathed the fresh air, trotting her horse. She wore an old pair of riding pants and a checked shirt under a sweater. Her short, curly white hair was held back with a narrow ribbon.

At her side rode Wellington. They were on the Avalanche Ranch. The ranch, in Helena, Montana, belonged to Wellington. Brother and sister were deep in conversation.

"You'll have my backing," said Wellington. "If you run."

"I'd have to have it," said Jeannette bluntly. "I have no money of my own. But—will I have the people's backing?"

It was a good question. It had been twenty years since Jeannette had lived in Montana. She was no longer well known in the state, at least to young voters. She'd come back to Montana now, in 1939, to try to learn two things. One was how Montanans felt about the U.S. getting into a war. The other was how they felt about sending Jeannette Rankin to the U.S. Congress.

A year earlier, Jeannette had given notice to the National Council. She'd gone on doing its work, anyway, until she could decide what else to do. In the end, it was events in Europe that led her to consider running for Congress. They were events that had been developing over a long period of time.

Most important among the events was the rise of the German dictator Adolph Hitler. He and his Nazi party had taken over Germany in 1933. At that time, with half the work force unemployed, the German people were in great misery. Hitler blamed their problems on Jews, Gypsies, Catholics, Communists, trade unions, gays and lesbians. Members of these groups were taken away to prison camps. Huge numbers were killed. Jews were Hitler's special target. He planned to wipe them out completely.

He also planned to take over all of Europe. He began by taking back land Germany had lost to France after World War I. Next, his troops overran Austria and Czechoslovakia.

Finally, on September 1, 1939, Hitler's troops invaded Poland. It was then that England and France declared war on Germany. Italy sided with Hitler. (The Soviet Union fought against Germany later, in 1941.) World War II had begun.

These events were enough to make Jeannette want to have a seat in Congress again. She believed that in Congress she could do the most to keep the U.S. from entering the war. Like other pacifists, she believed that nothing good came from people killing other people. War only increased the misery, the poverty, the hatreds that led to war in the first place.

Jeannette decided to start her campaign right away. There was a whole year before election time. But, she told Wellington, "The sooner I know whether or not I've got a chance, the better."

She began by talking to teenagers—even though they couldn't vote. She gave speeches at fifty-two of the fifty-six high schools in her voting district. White-haired as she was, the young people still took to her. She spoke simply and honestly; she made them laugh. She told the girls that with women voting, the day of a woman President was not far away. When the boys groaned, she said: "New opportunities are ahead for boys, too. Someday one of you may get to be the husband of a President." There was startled laughter, then applause.

The heart of her talk was always an appeal to students to help keep the U.S. out of war. As a former Congresswoman, she urged that it was important for them to write elected officials about their views. She advised them not to reveal themselves as teenagers. "You don't have to lie. Just don't tell them your age. *I* never do." There was more laughter, more applause.

Jeannette ended by asking students to talk these ideas over with their parents. In this way, she got her peace message into a lot of homes. She also made her name familiar all over the district. It was smart advertising—and cheaper than most.

Jeannette visited people in town and countryside, at home and on the job. Speaking on the radio, she was nearly as appealing as in person. It was on radio that she laid out her basic platform. That was before she'd announced that she was going to run for Congress. But she didn't change anything later. She didn't want voters to have any false impressions of her.

She made plain her belief that Hitler, and all he stood for, must be opposed. But she didn't believe that war was the way to do this. Wars didn't stop violence, she said. They created more violence. You couldn't stop Hitler's violent methods by adopting them, said Jeannette.

In fact, few Americans ever tried to do anything about Hitler's crimes. Only a handful of Jewish, Christian, and pacifist groups made any efforts to save his victims. Since 1933, these groups had been pleading for Jews to be let into the U.S. from Europe. That could be done if the President led Congress to make a change in immigration policy. But the President and Congress turned a deaf ear to these pleas. Millions of Jews, with nowhere to flee, were trapped and murdered. The war against Germany saved very few of them.

Jeannette thought the U.S. ought to stop sending arms overseas, and she said so. A lot of Americans agreed with her. They feared being drawn into Europe's wars.

At the same time, Jeannette believed that the U.S. should protect itself from invasion. Her position was: "Prepare to the limit to defend our rights and shores. Tell the world we won't send our men to fight in foreign wars."

Jeannette didn't think the U.S. was in much danger of outside attack, however. The real enemies of the nation, she said, were internal. They were unemployment, hunger, disease, the neglect of children and the aged. She pledged that she would continue working to overcome these tragic problems.

Jeannette's Democratic opponent, a U.S. Congressman, had a very good record of working on these problems, too. He didn't differ from her much about avoiding war, either. He had the support of a popular Democratic president, Franklin D. Roosevelt. Jeannette ran as a Republican. Finally, Jeannette's opponent was young. Jeannette was sixty.

All the same:

On November 5, 1940, Jeannette Rankin was elected for the second time to the U.S. House of Representatives. It wasn't even close. She won 56,616 to 47,352.

• • •

When Jeannette went to Congress the second time, some journalists wrote that women were no longer so unusual there. This claim wasn't true. In 1941, there were only seven women in the U.S. Congress—to 524 men. There had never been more than nine women at any one time since 1920. That was the year women had won the right to vote nationwide.

Jeannette wasn't thinking about any of this now. Her mind was taken up with the growing push toward war. In Congress, she set out to fight it immediately. She knew she had the backing of Montana voters. Hadn't she run, and won, on a peace platform?

Only a few weeks after taking office, she offered an amendment to the huge military bill. Her amendment said that U.S. armed forces could not be sent overseas without special approval from Congress. She didn't want the President to slip the military into action behind the people's backs.

When her amendment was voted down, she simply leaped back into the battle through another door. On May 6, she offered a resolution that would have the same effect as the amendment:

Congress hereby declares that it is the policy of the United States not to send the armed forces of the United States to fight in any place outside the Western Hemisphere or insular possessions of the United States.

This, too, was defeated. Congress and country had made a definite shift into a more warlike mood.

Jeannette didn't give up. Thereafter, she offered one measure after another to keep the nation from war. On November 28, she introduced a new kind of resolution. It was to hold a national election to find out if the people wanted war. If such an election were to be held, she felt sure of the outcome. "People never make war," she said. "It is always governments."

Of course, no such election had ever been held. This one wasn't held, either. The shocking events of December 7, 1941, kept Jeannette's resolution even from being considered.

More than a year earlier, Japan had come into the war on the side of Germany and Italy. After that, relations between Japan and the U.S. went downhill. Still, most Americans were surprised when Japanese warplanes bombed Pearl Harbor, the U.S. naval base near Honolulu, Hawaii. Almost 2,500 U.S. sailors were killed.

When Jeannette heard the terrible news she was on a train, traveling to a speaking date. She learned from the radio that the President was to address both houses of Congress the next day. He would ask for a declaration of war, she knew.

Early the next morning, Monday, December 8, she left the train. She boarded another train back to Washington, D.C.

It was as if her life were repeating itself. But a lot had changed since the first World War. Especially, Jeannette Rankin had changed. She hated war and violence even more, now that she knew more about them. She was also more sure of herself.

In her apartment, the phone was ringing. It was

Wellington. "Please, don't—" he began. She said: "You know it's no use asking me, dear." Wellington was silenced. His influence on Jeannette, he knew, wasn't what it had been in the past. There really was no use in trying to talk her into voting for war. He said goodbye quietly.

When Jeannette entered the House chambers, her face was pale and grim. This time, unlike 1917, she knew that she was truly alone. Not a voice against war was going to be raised in the nation's Capitol. None, that is, unless she raised hers.

The minute the war resolution was read, she was on her feet. "Mr. Speaker, I object—" she began; but the House Speaker ruled her out of order. He then allowed several representatives to speak, before a vote was asked for. "Mr. Speaker, I would like to be heard!" cried Jeannette. Ignoring her, the speaker asked for the roll call of "ayes" and "nays."

Jeannette was frantic. What! No debate at all? For the third time, she cried out to be heard. "Mr. Speaker, a point of order!" This time, she was heard by radio news reporters. They had set up a microphone at the speaker's podium. She was also heard by people packed into the halls outside the chambers.

Now some of the "gentlemen" of the House roared, "Sit down, sister!" The roll call began. Jeannette sank back into her seat. But when "Rankin" was called, she stood. "Nay!" she cried, in a voice that was loud and clear. Comments weren't supposed to be made during roll calls, but she added: "As a woman I cannot go to war, and I refuse to send anyone else."

Unlike 1917, not one member of Congress voted "nay" except Jeannette. While her vote, back then, had drawn some admiring applause, now there were only boos and hisses. Things got worse when she left the chambers. In the hall, a group of army officers surrounded her, yelling and cursing. She sniffed their breath. "Why, you've been drinking!" she exclaimed.

Beyond them, a menacing mob moved toward her. Pushing past the officers, Jeannette slipped into a phone booth. Coolly she dialed a number. In a few minutes the Capitol police arrived. They escorted her to her office, where she worked behind locked doors all afternoon. A guard in uniform kept watch outside.

The hatred shown by the mob soon showed itself in letters.

> **Why in hell don't you leave that job—you disgrace the office you hold—damn you.**
>
> **You are an old fossil. Never should you have been an official of any kind—rather an undertaker's assistant for women only.**
>
> **You are the only living argument against giving unmarried women the vote.**
>
> **You made an ass out of yourself trying to be like a man. Now come home like a lady.**
>
> **Did the Nazis promise you a husband for your vote?**
>
> **Pig Rankin. Bitch Rankin. Traitor Nazi. Jap. Skunk.**

With enormous dignity, Jeannette responded to every letter. She bore the filth heaped upon her without being dirtied by it.

At sixty, Jeannette no longer wavered about doing what she thought was right. Her moral standards, formed over so many years, out of so many political conflicts, gave her no choice. Explaining her vote to the chairman of NCPW, she wrote:

What one decides to do in a crisis depends upon one's philosophy in life, and that philosophy cannot be changed by an accident. If one hasn't any philosophy, in crises others make the decision. The most disappointing feature of working for a cause is that so few people have a clear philosophy of life. We used to say, in the suffrage movement, that we could trust the woman who believed in suffrage, but we could never trust the woman who just wanted to vote.

Only a few people understood the stand Jeannette took. Even among those, however, no more than a handful went so far as to praise her. Outstanding among them was Lillian Smith, best known today as the author of the novel *Strange Fruit*. A white Southerner, of Jeannette's adopted state of Georgia, Smith herself was a woman of unusual strength. She had long fought against injustice and inhumanity toward her black fellow-citizens. Of Jeannette's act, Smith wrote: "That one little vote of yours stands out like a bright star in a dark night."

Jeannette went bravely back into the dark night, to finish her term in Congress. She battled against fraud and waste in the billions of dollars being poured into the war effort. She struggled to ease some of the hardships caused by the military draft. She tried to get direct relief for American Indian families whose men had been drafted, leaving the women with no way to make ends meet. "These are the most needy people in the whole country," she pleaded.

In this, as in most efforts now, she failed. Most House members were thrilled that the war boom was making lots of jobs. They were busy rushing still more war bills through the House. If a few people weren't profiting, just too bad, they thought.

Americans were now strongly united behind the war effort. Jeannette didn't seem like much of a danger. Even when she charged that the Roosevelt administration had provoked the bombing of Pearl Harbor, she drew little outcry. (Thirty years later, secret British documents revealed facts that gave added weight to her charges.) Little by little, the attacks on her died down. By the time her term ended, she said years later, she was "just ignored."

CHAPTER 9

Journeys

It was quite a while before Jeannette returned to live in Georgia. When she packed up and left Congress the second time, she went back to Montana. Wellington was thinking of running for the U.S. Senate again. He'd always helped her in politics. So she wanted to be on hand to help him. Also, by 1943 Jeannette's mother was over ninety. She needed a lot of care, which the family had been sharing. It was Jeannette's turn to do her part.

Wellington did decide to run for Senator. Jeannette enjoyed the excitement of working in his campaign. But when he lost to his Democratic opponent, she became depressed. For the first time, she faced the thought that *she* probably couldn't win re-election. Certainly not while a war she opposed was going on.

Except in letters to friends, Jeannette now said little against the war. Neither did thousands of others who, for years, had worked tirelessly to try to prevent it. The war had become popular with many who had once supported the cause of peace. People of good will, they were horrified by the brutality of the Nazis and their allies. At last, they saw no way of stopping it except through armed force. The peace movement was shattered.

Only the true pacifist groups stuck by their belief that

all wars were wrong. Even they, however, made it clear that they would in no way interfere with the U.S. war effort. These groups worked legally to protect pacifist men from having to enter the military. Classed as "conscientious objectors" (CO's), the men were put into civilian prison camps. There they did hard labor, without pay. A few thousand of the CO's refused to cooperate with the war in any way. They walked away from the camps, or didn't register for the draft to begin with. They were punished—as they expected to be—with federal prison.

This period of World War II was the low point of Jeannette Rankin's life. The peace movement she'd helped to build was now a bare shadow. Her career in that movement and in Congress had ground to a halt. She was no longer a woman of public affairs, with public duties. Her duties were the private, family kind, traditional for women. Overnight, her status had changed, from daring politician to "old maid" daughter caring for her mother. Even the roof over her head wasn't hers. It was Wellington's.

Jeannette had a house of her own, of course. It was on a farm near Watkinsville, Georgia. (Her first house, near Athens, had burned down.) She went there a few times during the war. She was remodeling the only building on the farm, an old shanty.

Mostly, however, Jeannette sat out World War II in Montana. She had a fair amount of time to herself. Olive Rankin's needs were partly attended to by a paid household helper. Jeannette used her spare time to read and think.

For many years, she had been interested in the ideas of Mahatma Gandhi, the great Hindu leader of India. He was fighting to win freedom for his country from Great

Britain, ruler over all of India since 1858. Jeannette began to study carefully Gandhi's use of peaceful methods to bring about basic changes. While his final goal was India's independence from Great Britain, his people didn't try to reach this goal through armed struggle. Their tactics were peaceful ones, such as protest marches, boycotts, strikes, and picketing.

Their most powerful weapon was their refusal to obey unjust laws. For example, the British made laws against protest marches. But the people, defying the laws, marched anyway. They were willing to go to jail for it. This open law-breaking, called "civil disobedience," was later used in the U.S. civil rights struggle led by Dr. Martin Luther King, Jr. It helped African-Americans win rights they had been denied since slavery. For while the U.S. Civil War had freed them from slavery, it had not brought them equal rights.

Jeannette couldn't foresee Dr. King's movement, which at that time was ten years in the future. But she was desperately seeking answers to the problem of war. Especially wars that had started like World War II! What could you do against evils such as Nazism? Were the only choices to let them continue—or to adopt violence, just like your opponent?

Gandhi's methods offered a way to struggle against evil without using violence. Jeannette made up her mind that she would go to India, to observe that struggle, at her first chance. That chance came in 1946. By then, there were two trained nurses looking after her mother. Also, because the war was over, foreign travel was easier.

The war had ended in a way that was beyond Jeannette's worst nightmares. With Germany defeated in the spring of 1945, Japan fought on. Then, on August 6,

1945, U.S. President Harry Truman ordered an atomic bomb blasted over Hiroshima, Japan. It was the first atomic bomb in history. Its power to destroy was terrible. In a flash, nearly the entire city was leveled to the ground. Over 160,000 people were killed outright or injured. In time, thousands more died of the effects of radiation.

Two days later, the U.S. dropped a second atomic bomb, on Nagasaki, Japan. Another 80,000 were killed or injured. After that, Japan surrendered.

Neither Hiroshima nor Nagasaki was a military target. They were cities filled with children, old people, women, and men not in uniform. At this time, the U.S. was the only country in the world capable of making an atomic bomb. It set the world a cruel example by using it against helpless civilians.

Soon, many other nations would join in the race for "the bomb." Jeannette was among those who saw that the nuclear weapons race threatened to end the human race. As she set sail for India, that threat was in her mind.

In spite of her grave thoughts, Jeannette was excited to be traveling again. At sixty-six, her zest for new adventures was fresh as ever. Fearlessly she set off across India, driving her own car, which came by ship. She had contacts in a lot of places, but often preferred to be on her own. Wherever she went, she spent time talking with strangers. Asking many questions, she learned all she could about the lives of ordinary people.

She arrived at New Delhi, the capital of India, after two months on the road. There, she learned that Gandhi was leaving, on foot, early the next morning. His purpose was to make peace between two quarreling religious groups, Hindus and Moslems. Not wishing to disturb him at such a time, Jeannette put off meeting him. She didn't get another chance. Before she visited India again, he was killed by an assassin.

While in New Delhi, Jeannette attended the first public meeting of the All-India Congress. Jeannette was known as a friend to India's freedom. She was welcomed warmly by Congress members. The British had only recently released the Congress members from prison, where they had been held because of their leadership in the Indian struggle. The following year, 1947, Britain was to grant India full independence. Jeannette met with the president of the Congress. She also met with Jawaharlal Nehru, who became India's first prime minister.

This trip was the first of seven that Jeannette was to make to India. It was also the start of journeys that would occupy her for the next twenty years. Besides India, her travels included Indonesia, Africa, Mexico, South America, Western Europe, Russia, and Turkey. After 1965, most of her travels were in the U.S. But she took a final trip to India at age ninety.

She didn't expect to learn much about a country and its people without discomfort. Blessed with good health, she was ready for the chances of the road. One of her nieces recalled:

> **She would stay anywhere, without ever grumbling about [housing] or food, unless there wasn't any. I only heard her complain once: she had boarded a freighter for a six week return from India, and no one aboard spoke English!**

Jeannette's accounts of herself were not always as kind as her niece's. When she visited India the second time, after nursing her mother through her final illness, she attended a 1949 World Pacifist Conference. She and some other visitors were housed at Gandhi's last home. Gandhi had believed in living as poorly as the poorest Indian. Jeannette humorously reported:

> **Imagine my dismay when I found the bed was made of hard boards and nothing else! All I had was a cotton saree and wool blanket. Someone found me a thin quilt and mat.**

What was Jeannette seeking in her twenty-year, round-the-world journey? She who had been a leader and a teacher in the field of peace had become a student. She was in search of answers to the problem of war. For the problem was more urgent than it had ever been. The new nuclear weapons threatened to destroy the earth. Yet nations went on following the same old military paths. They were not really even trying to avoid wars.

The U.S. was hardly out of World War II before it began fighting a war in Korea. By the time that war ended, in 1953, it had taken 38,000 American lives alone. U.S. leaders said that the Soviet Union planned to take over the world. The U.S. policy was therefore to oppose Soviet communism all over the world. That was the reason given for the Korean War. That was also the reason given for the endless U.S. military build-up.

As these events were going on, Jeannette's views were changing. She no longer believed that the U.S. should arm for self-defense. She thought it should disarm completely. She shared Gandhi's view that sooner or later, a person who has a gun will use it. Much better not to have the gun to begin with—especially if the "gun" is a nuclear bomb! In short, Jeannette had come to think that the U.S. should disarm right away, altogether, and without waiting for other nations to do the same.

This was a radical view, held by only a few pacifist groups in the U.S. In this period, however, Jeannette didn't have much to do with those groups, or any other U.S. peace groups. For some years, she quietly "dropped out" of the U.S. peace movement.

Perhaps Jeannette needed to turn away for a while from the U.S. peace movement. There was reason enough for her to feel tired of it. She once said, "I worked for suffrage for years, and got it. I've worked for peace for fifty-five years and haven't come close." Another time, during the Korean War, she told Katherine Anthony that she felt her life had been futile. Her work, she said, had served no purpose. Her friend protested:

I am not going to allow you to say that. That just isn't true. With all that you have accomplished in life you should never let such a thought enter your mind.

Not long after this, the public was reminded of Jeannette's accomplishments. In 1958, U.S. Senator John F. Kennedy, who later became president, published an article titled "Three Women of Courage." In it, he praised Jeannette Rankin as one of the most courageous figures in American history. "Few members of Congress have ever stood more alone," he wrote, for being "true to a higher honor and loyalty."

It was President Kennedy's policies that led to the next stage in Jeannette's active political life. For it was he who sent ever-greater numbers of U.S. troops to Vietnam. By the time of his assassination, in 1963, the U.S. was tangled in a huge new war, against Vietnam. Jeannette began to speak out.

Her views were still news. Coming home from her

travels—whether she landed in Georgia, Montana, or elsewhere—she was interviewed by the local press. In her anti-war stand, she was *not* alone now. The Vietnam War was less and less popular.

As Jeannette's foreign trips became fewer, her interviews in the press became more frequent. Impressed by her comments, a group called Atlantans for Peace asked her to speak at a public meeting. At eighty-seven, she hadn't given a formal speech for twenty years. She asked herself, *why not?*—and quickly accepted.

On May 18, 1967, about seventy-five people gathered at a church for Jeannette's speech. The Atlanta meeting was only one of hundreds of protests going on in the country. Yet Jeannette's speech made national headlines. This veteran of the suffrage movement called upon *women* to stop the war.

Ten thousand boys have died in Vietnam. I predict that if 10,000 American women had mind enough they could end the war, if they were committed to the task, even if it meant going to jail. You cannot have wars without the women.

The main theme of Jeannette's speech was an old one, for her. But it sent a thrill through many women. Among them were members of Women Strike for Peace (WSP), a group that had been struggling against war since the early 1960s. They had shown their bravery, often standing alone. Still, it fired their courage to feel that they were supported by this great hero out of women's past. Some women were learning about her for the first time. Others knew her name, but thought that she'd died.

The answer to Jeannette's call for women's action wasn't long in coming. By summer, she was working with women on a giant protest against the war. Under the leadership of WSP, women around the country were organizing to march on Washington, D.C. They named themselves the Jeannette Rankin Brigade.

The leaders of the project hoped to attract the 10,000 women Jeannette had spoken of. However, they had no intention of anyone's going to jail. They knew that was too radical an idea for most people. To many, even joining a march was a scary idea. That was easy to understand. The police, these days, were quick to crack heads at even the most peaceful protests. Fears must be calmed if the march were to attract large numbers.

While some women working on the project worried about its *form*, most agreed on all its *aims*. Those aims could be seen in the petition the Jeannette Rankin Brigade would present to Congress. It called on Congress to do the following:

1. Resolve to end the war in Vietnam and immediately withdraw all American troops.
2. Use its power to heal a sick society at home.
3. Use its power to restore the ruined land we leave behind in Vietnam.
4. Listen to what the American people are saying and refuse to bow to the demands of military/industrial leaders.

Jeannette completely supported the petition. And what of her call for going to jail? She was not bitter that it had not been taken up. She knew that for some women it was a very big thing just to march in the streets. Everybody had to begin somewhere, she thought. Even Jeannette Rankin, whose marching had begun a long time ago, hadn't risked jail.

The streets of the capital were quiet and snow-filled on the morning of the march. It was January 15, 1968. The sun peeped in and out. The women gathered early at Union Station. It looked like a huge crowd. Observers didn't agree on the numbers. Five thousand, the police said; ten thousand, others reported. Jeannette was to walk at the head of the march. Nearby were march organizer Vivian Hallinan; folk singer Judy Collins; civil rights leader Coretta King; and the wives of the only two U.S. Senators firmly against the war. There were a few children.

Now the women in front unrolled their long banner. They held it in front of them. It said: "End the War in Vietnam and Social Crisis at Home!" And now the marshall of the march nodded her head at Jeannette and said, "The Jeannette Rankin Brigade is ready to go."

Jeannette nodded back. In her trim winter boots, she stepped out smartly. Her glasses caught a ray of sun. A smile lit up her wrinkled face.

Jeannette Rankin was marching again.

CHAPTER 10

Fly on, Dove of Peace

In her eighties, Jeannette didn't look so different from other middle-class, healthy white women of her age. She was lucky in having a back that was still straight. She'd always been on the slender side, and she still was. Sometimes, when the tinting of her hair turned out wrong, she wore a wig. Anyone who looked closely could tell it was a wig. It was more glossy than her own hair. Her face was kind and cheerful.

In short, as a friend of hers said, Jeannette looked to most people like "a harmless little old lady." Her friend added, with a laugh: "She's not. She's a ball of fire!"

After the 1968 women's march on Washington, the "ball of fire" was in great demand as a speaker. Letters, telegrams, and phone calls came streaming to the farm near Watkinsville, Georgia. Requests to speak came from women's groups, anti-war groups, youth groups. They came from every part of the country. Jeannette tried to accept every one of them. During this time, a reporter asked her where she lived. Was it in Montana or Georgia? Jeannette said, "I live in an airplane."

But she loved it. And audiences loved her. She was even a hero to youth. This was in a time when youth did not trust age. College men had begun to be drafted, along

with men who came from poorer families. The middle-
class young now became angry at their parents and other
adults. The adults had done nothing to stop the Vietnam
War! But the anger included older people in the anti-war
movement, too. "Don't trust anybody over thirty" was
the saying.

Jeannette was among the few who were trusted. A
poster with her photo was popular in "hippie" shops and
bookstores. In October 1969, she spoke at an all-day anti-
war meeting at the University of Georgia. There were
many speakers that day. But it was Jeannette for whom
the audience of 1500 rose to its feet, cheering. In the following months, the same thing happened at other colleges
and universities where she spoke.

She understood and shared the rage of the young. For
their lives were being wasted, thrown away—again! Once
a reporter asked for her views about campus violence.
Her reply was: "If a nation sends boys halfway around the
world to be shot, can you blame a few little boys for
throwing stones?"

Jeannette's own travels around the world weren't yet
over, busy as she was at home. In 1969 she visited Czechoslovakia. She planned to go next to Russia, where she'd
been once before. But in March 1970, a couple of months
before she was to leave, she had a fall. She slipped on the
Watkinsville drugstore steps.

One person after another rushed over to her.
Jeannette, who guessed she'd broken her hip, asked not to
be touched. She asked that expert help be sent, to move
her to the hospital.

Directing everyone, Jeannette was cool as lemonade.
As she was about to be carried off, a bystander saw an odd
object on the sidewalk. "What's that thing?" he said.

"My wig," Jeannette said calmly. "Let's have it."

She was nearly ninety, an age when a broken hip is serious. Jeannette was upset for a special reason. Friends were planning a ninetieth birthday dinner for her, in the nation's capital. She didn't want to let them down, by being bedridden in Georgia. She had until June 11, to recover.

Her aim was to get to the party on her own two feet. She worked hard at it, using a walker. She also went on working at other projects. She answered mail and phone calls. She taped a speech for the Rankin Rank and File. This was an anti-war group in New York that she'd earlier promised to address.

In spite of her efforts, Jeannette still needed a wheelchair when she flew to Washington, D.C. Yet she was radiant, as she entered the Rayburn House Office Building on June 11, 1970.

Two hundred people had come together to honor her. There were peace and human rights leaders, other friends, and family members. Jeannette sat between Senators Mike Mansfield and Lee Metcalf, of Montana. Also at the main table was Representative Patsy T. Mink, of Hawaii, a strong opponent of the war, and an effective worker for women's rights. And Senator Margaret Chase Smith, of Maine, was there, one of the rare women ever elected to the U.S. Senate.

Senator Smith spoke of Jeannette's powerful impact on her own thinking. A few days before, the Senate had defeated a measure that could have broadened the war. It would have let President Nixon send troops to Vietnam's neighbor country of Cambodia, without Congress's consent.

Everyone knew that Senator Smith was a "hawk"—one who supported the war. Yet she had cast her vote with the Senate's "peace doves," thus helping to defeat the measure. This, she said, showed "Miss Rankin's influence." Said Senator Smith: "She broke the way for me by being elected in 1916. I salute her for being the original dove in Congress."

Senator Metcalf praised Jeannette for being ahead of her time. Among many other examples, he spoke of her early interest in child welfare, labor problems, social and racial injustice, American Indian rights. "These all sound like a reading of the calendar of issues before the Congress today," he said.

When it was Jeannette's turn to speak, she stood, rising from her wheelchair. At ninety, she soon had her audience spellbound. Her mind was keen. Alone among the speakers, she used no written speech, or even notes. She was also the only one to speak of the future, more than the past.

That was the case in the next days, too, when there were more interviews than ever. She looked forward to a future when there would be many women in public office. "We're half the people. We should be half the Congress," she declared.

"War is nonsense," she told a *San Francisco Examiner* reporter, "bring the boys back now." Another reporter asked her, how were we to get the boys home? "The same way we got them in," snapped Jeannette. "By ships and planes." Asked whether this wouldn't be surrender, she said: "Surrender is a military idea. When you're doing something wrong, you stop."

Asked to comment on racism, she compared it to prejudice against women. She said that all the arguments against equality for black people had first been used against women.

Jeannette had not taken an active part in the Southern civil rights movement led by Dr. Martin Luther King, Jr. The height of that movement had occurred during the years when Jeannette was seldom in the U.S. It was during that same period that she "dropped out" of the U.S. peace movement. Nevertheless, she was known as a good friend to civil rights. Dr. King's widow, Coretta King, sending Jeannette greetings on her ninetieth birthday, said, "It has been a privilege to support your efforts and to have my efforts supported by so great a woman."

Living in Georgia, Jeannette was constantly surrounded by racism. Yet she didn't give it the attention she gave other issues. Except when asked for her views, she seldom made a direct comment on it. Meanwhile, she went on living according to her own values. On her Georgia farm property, she built a comfortable modern house for the black caretaker, his wife and children. Jeannette herself was content to live in the old cabin that she slowly remodeled over the years. If others found such reverse inequality odd, that didn't bother Jeannette.

She was a backer of Shirley Chisholm, a black Congress member, in Chisholm's 1972 campaign for the U.S. presidency. Chisholm's color wasn't a factor in Jeannette's choice. To Jeannette, Chisholm was simply the best candidate. She helped kick off Chisholm's campaign in Georgia, with a dinner speech in Atlanta. In this public act, it was clear that Jeannette stood apart from the white racist society around her.

Of course, Jeannette had stood apart no matter where she was. Because she was outspoken, critics in Montana had called her "self-willed." That had been years before. By the time of Chisholm's campaign, Jeannette was ninety-two. She said whatever she wanted to say—and did as much as she could.

That was still a lot. By now, she had a secretary to keep her many appointments straight. He was a law student named John Kirkley. Being her secretary had been his own idea. He was one of the young people who admired Jeannette. In 1971, he started to visit her on his motorbike. He offered to do some typing, then some cooking and housekeeping. After a while, it seemed to make sense for him to move in.

There was room for Kirkley now. With remodeling, the tiny cabin had grown to four rooms. The place had a few more modern comforts than Jeannette's first Georgia farmhouse. There was electricity, instead of oil lamps. With water piped into the house, there was an indoor toilet and bathtub. However, Jeannette never put in a pump. So the toilet had to be flushed with a jug filled at the tap in the tub. Hot water for baths came from a kettle heated on the old-fashioned kitchen stove.

Jeannette's family and close friends worried about the dangers of this house. They asked Jeannette why she didn't modernize more. Sometimes she answered that she'd rather spend the money on travel. Or she would say that any extra money of hers went to important causes.

But the truth was that Jeannette no longer had to count her pennies. Years before, Wellington had given her a ranch in Montana. She drew an income from this. He gave her a retirement home in California, too. His death, in 1966, left her well-off.

Jeannette may have lived as she did for reasons something like Gandhi's. Unlike Gandhi, she was not religious.

Even so, she didn't like to depend a lot on the material things of this world. And, like Gandhi, she probably didn't want a life too far above the hard daily lives of the poor.

In reality, Jeannette didn't spend much time in her four-room Georgia cabin. More often, she was living "in an airplane." It was a remarkable life for a woman her age. The National Organization for Women (NOW) was laying plans to honor her entire remarkable life. The country's leading feminist organization, NOW had voted to name Jeannette to its Susan B. Anthony Hall of Fame. Jeannette would be the first to receive an award as "the world's outstanding living feminist," on February 14, 1972.

The award ceremony came in the midst of a rush of other activities. In the weeks before and after it, Jeannette spoke at political meetings in Georgia, Tennessee, Arkansas, Montana, and New York. She appeared on the David Frost TV show. She was interviewed on the TODAY show and on the Dick Cavett show. *Ms.* magazine, the *New York Times*, and *Life* printed interviews.

The *Times* writer asked her what she'd do if she could live her life again. Jeannette said she'd do everything the same, except for one thing. "This time," she said, "I'd be nastier."

The NOW ceremony was held at a New York hotel. Most of the women who sat waiting for Jeannette were young. Jeannette was a living link between them and a heroic past. She connected early suffragists like Susan B. Anthony with their world of new feminism. When she walked in, brisk, erect, and lively, there was a moment's stunned quiet. Then the room burst into applause. Jeannette's eyes filled with sudden tears. But she did not falter. With her usual poise and energy, she began to speak. Her main thrust was for the future.

Women must devote all their energies today in gaining enough political offices to influence the direction of government.... We are here together to work together for the elimination of war.... My dream has always been that women would take this responsibility.

My dream.... Indeed, it was a dream. There was not much to base it on. There was no reason to believe, in 1972, that women would catch up with men in political office-holding soon. (Twenty years later, in the election "Year of the Woman," men still kept 94 percent of U.S. Senate seats and 89 percent of the House.) Nor was there any reason to think that women, even if they won "enough political offices," would oppose wars. So far, there had been only a few female "doves" in Congress.

But as Jeannette's words flowed to her listeners, that hardly mattered. What mattered was that Jeannette believed it—most of the time. Jeannette's dreams had not kept her from facing hard political facts. Yet her dreams had helped her rise above the facts, striving for something better, and taking others with her. Behind her politics lay her dreams.

· · ·

Jeannette's dreams were still fresh and growing when she died. That was on May 18, 1973. Less than a year before, reformer Ralph Nader had praised her creative approach to political problems. In a study of former Congress members, he asked for their ideas for congressional reforms. He reported:

The most spirited and fundamental response came from Jeannette Rankin. . . . If aging is the erosion of one's ideals, then Jeannette Rankin is young forever.

Yet even Jeannette was mortal. She and Nader met just before her health began to fail. A problem with the muscles of her throat made eating hard for her. Her weight dropped. Worse for her, her speech was affected. It was a trial not to be able to make herself understood.

She had been spending winters at her Carmel, California, retirement home. Now she stayed on, for the handy medical services. Her sister Edna and friends also lived nearby. Jeannette wrote letters, read, and watched TV, trying to keep up with public affairs. One night, in her sleep, her heart failed.

Her ashes were scattered over the sea. News of her death, flashing around the world, meant little to most. But for those who continue the long struggle for justice and peace, Jeannette Rankin remains an inspiration.

The spirit of the valiant dove flies on.

JEANNETTE PICKERING RANKIN
(1880–1973)

Outline of Life Events

June 11, 1880. Born on a ranch in Missoula, Montana. Oldest of six girls (five survive past childhood) and one boy, Wellington.

1902–04. Graduates University of Montana, at age twenty-two, with B.S. in biology. Teaches grade school, then works as dressmaker in Missoula. Visits Boston slums and is shocked by urban poverty. Begins to read protest literature.

1908–10. Attends New York School of Philanthropy. Works at orphan home in Spokane, Washington. Attends University of Washington, Seattle. Works in successful Washington campaign to pass state woman suffrage amendment.

1911–13. Makes speech urging woman suffrage before Montana legislature. National suffrage leaders recognize her talent for political work. Gets job with New York Woman Suffrage Party. Travels country for National American Woman Suffrage Association.

1914–15. Directs successful campaign for suffrage amendment in Montana. With outbreak of World War I, participates in founding of Woman's Peace Party. Travels to

New Zealand to study effects of women's voting power in that country.

1916. Runs for U.S. Congress as a Republican, and wins.

1917–19. Votes against U.S. entry into World War I, despite huge pressure for a yes vote. Defeated in next election. While still in Congress, plays major role in bringing before the House a Constitutional amendment for nationwide woman suffrage. (Amendment passed by both houses in 1920.) Atends Women's Peace Meeting in Zurich, Switzerland. Co-founder there of Women's International League for Peace and Freedom (WILPF).

1920–24. Works as lobbyist for National Consumers League.

1923. Moves, builds house in farm country near Athens, Georgia.

1925–29. Accepts job with WILPF. Sets up Georgia Peace Society. Works for Women's Peace Union, lobbying Congress for passage of Constitutional amendment to outlaw war.

1929–1939. For nearly ten years, holds job as lobbyist and field secretary for National Council for the Prevention of War.

1939. At age sixty, begins second campaign for Congress. Wins.

1940–43. Day after Pearl Harbor, casts the only vote in Congress against U.S. entry into World War II. Public fury unleashed against her; loses any chances of reelection. Spends term mostly on war issues, such as military draft exemptions and war profiteering.

1943–46. Returns to Montana to help family with care of elderly mother. Studies nonviolence as practiced by Gandhi's movement in India. Begins world travel, seeking answers to problem of war. When in U.S., makes Georgia her home again.

1946–1967. Goes to India (returning there six times), Western and Eastern Europe, Mideast, Asia, Africa, Mexico, South America. Observes lives of ordinary people, attends international conferences. Becomes an absolute pacifist, taking position for total, universal disarmament. In mid-1960s, begins speaking out loudly against Vietnam War.

1967–1971. In Atlanta, Georgia, gives widely reported speech against Vietnam War. Peace movement and women's movement begin to seek her out. **January 15, 1968,** leads the Jeannette Rankin Brigade in its Washington, D.C. demonstration against the Vietnam War. Lobbies Congress against the war, speaks and works against war all over the country. **June 11, 1970,** attends U.S. House celebration of her ninetieth birthday.

February 12, 1972. Delivers rousing speech in ceremony at which National Organization for Women (NOW) names her the first member of the Susan B. Anthony Hall of Fame.

May 18, 1973. Dies, Carmel, California, at nearly ninety-three.

PATSY T. MINK

The Takemoto family, 1932 or 1933. Patsy Takemoto Mink was about five years old at the time this photo was made. Left to right, Suematsu, Eugene, Mitama Tateyama, Patsy.

January 3, 1965. Wearing a victory smile, Patsy T. Mink is sworn into Congress by Speaker of the House John W. McCormack. She was the first Asian-American woman and the first woman of color to be elected to Congress.

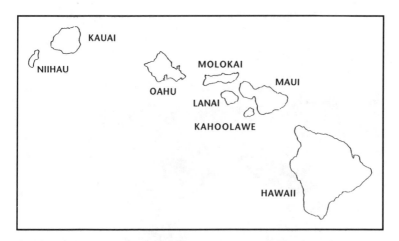

The State of Hawaii is a group of islands in the Pacific Ocean, 2400 miles southwest of the U.S. mainland. Patsy T. Mink was born and grew up on Maui. Today her Congressional district includes part of Oahu plus all the other islands of Hawaii.

Patsy T. Mink in her Washington, D.C. office, 1970. With her are her daughter, Wendy, and her husband, John. Her family has always strongly supported her political career.

As a member of Congress, Patsy T. Mink has worked tirelessly for peace, women's rights, civil rights, and other efforts to promote justice and equality. When she makes a public statement, as in this 1971 photo, she leaves no doubt about where she stands.

CHAPTER 1

Not Quite Paradise

In a tropical garden, a family of three smiles happily at the camera. Mother (Patsy), father (John), and daughter (Wendy), wear matching T-shirts. The T-shirts say:

"Think Mink. U.S. Congress."

The picture was taken for a news magazine, in 1965. At that time, Patsy Takemoto Mink had won her first race for the U.S. House of Representatives. She was going to represent Hawaii, the nation's youngest state. At thirty-seven, she would be the youngest member in Congress. She was also the first Asian-American woman ever to be elected to Congress.

The small woman smiling out of the picture had always had high aims. She always felt that if she worked hard, her aims would succeed. Yet her path in life had not always been easy. There had been times of pure, golden joy. But there had been painful times, too.

There had even been times of terror.

• • •

Hawaii is a group of islands in the Pacific Ocean. The best-known of the islands are Oahu, Kauai, Maui, and Hawaii. Patsy Takemoto was born on Maui, on December 6,

1927. She grew up in a small Maui town known as Hamakuapoko.

At that time, there were about five hundred families in Hamakuapoko. Most people made their living by working for a sugar company. Sugar cane grew on huge farms called plantations. Almost everywhere you looked was the tall grass of the cane, waving like green waves of the sea.

In Patsy's little town, there were not many Native Hawaiians—that is, people whose ancestors were the first humans to live on the islands. Most people in Patsy's town were of Japanese, Filipino, or Portuguese descent. These groups had first been brought to Hawaii to work on the sugar plantations owned by rich white families. So had laborers from China, Korea, and Puerto Rico. The largest group of immigrants was the Japanese, who began arriving by the thousands in the 1880s.

Patsy's grandparents, on both sides, were among the Japanese immigrants. They found a hard, cruel life as plantation workers. Wages were low, hours were long. Bosses treated the workers without respect and sometimes beat them with whips. Patsy's mother's parents would not put up with that kind of life. They went to live in Maui's forest wilderness, making a home there.

Little Patsy and her brother, Eugene, often begged their mother to tell them about her early life. Their mother, Mitama Tateyama, was born in her parents' house in the wilderness. Most of her ten sisters and brothers were born there, too. In the years before Mr. Tateyama opened a little general store, the family lived on food gathered from the forest and the ocean. Patsy was deeply impressed by their brave struggle. All the Tateyama children, including Mitama, completed at least eight grades of school. Seven completed high school.

Most young people did not get that much schooling, at the time.

Patsy was very much attached to her gentle, strong mother. She also warmly admired her father, Suematsu Takemoto, a quiet, kind, hard-working man. He had a good position, as a land surveyor for an irrigation company. Orphaned as a small boy, he had worked his way through high school and through the University of Hawaii. In 1922, he became the first Japanese-American to graduate with a degree in civil engineering. Patsy felt sure that, like her father, she would go to college some day.

Patsy's interest in school began when she was about four. That was when Eugene, a year and a half older than Patsy, started school. The school was just across the road from the Takemotos' house. Patsy tagged after Eugene, who was her daily playmate. "She'll get tired of it soon," laughed the teacher and Patsy's parents. But instead, Patsy began to learn with the other children. By the time this became clear, it seemed a shame to hold Patsy back. She stayed in Eugene's grade.

Patsy and her brother had many friends who came to their house to play. It was a roomy house set on a big plot of land. Tropical fruit trees—mango, papaya, guava, and many others—made the air sweet. There were pet dogs and cats, and sometimes rabbits to care for. At the nearby beach, there were shells to find, and sand for tunnels and castles. There was always something to do. Baseball was a favorite game with the children. Patsy played with the boys, because Eugene put her on his team.

Patsy and Eugene's friends were mostly Japanese or Filipino, children of plantation workers. But Patsy also went often to play with the daughter of the irrigation company manager. The manager and his family were *haole*, as white people are called in the Hawaiian Islands. When Patsy was a grown woman, she recalled:

> **I learned at an early age how differently the "white" people lived. They ate different foods and even the chinaware looked different. I learned too that often-times their children did not eat their meals with their parents, but ate in the kitchen with their servants.**

To the child Patsy, it seemed a sad thing to eat apart from your parents. She especially loved the evening meal with her mother and father. She and Eugene had so much to tell, and their parents were always interested.

The family spent a lot of time together. They pic-nicked and swam at the beach. They worked together in their vegetable garden. Sometimes they saw a movie at the theater in Hamakuapoko. They seldom missed the county fair, where the children rode on the merry-go-round.

Like many families in the 1930s, the Takemotos en-joyed the radio. Sometimes Mr. and Mrs. Takemoto lis-tened to programs in Japanese. More often, they listened to English-language programs and to music. With Patsy and Eugene, they listened to family comedy programs.

When Patsy was five, the family began to listen to the broadcasts of the U.S. President, Franklin D. Roosevelt. The President called these programs "fireside chats." Patsy knew that these broadcasts were very important. Her father said that President Roosevelt was a great man. He said the President would pull the country out of the Depression. The President, said Mr. Takemoto, would improve the lives of all the American people.

Patsy was not able to understand the meaning of much that the President said. Yet the fireside chats thrilled her. The President had a way of speaking that was dramatic but warm. It seemed as if he were right there in the room. He seemed to be talking to the four Takemotos.

During the years of the fireside chats, Patsy sometimes heard people besides her father speak of the Depression. Sometimes she heard people talking about "bad times." At the movies, she saw newsreel pictures of people wearing ragged clothes. They shivered on snowy streets, waiting in line for free food. After a while, Patsy heard adults saying that "times" were better.

Patsy learned to make sense of all this by the time she reached her teens. She grasped the fact that millions of people had been needy and suffering. Yet it didn't seem quite real to her. Not only her own family, but nobody she knew had gone hungry. Most people grew their own vegetables and could fish from the sea. Heavy clothes were not needed, since winter is not cold in Hawaii. Hawaii's mild climate, its fruitful earth, its tropical beauty, have long made it known as "Paradise." For Patsy, it went right on being Paradise.

Thus in Hawaii's endless summer, Patsy grew up. She was a small, pretty girl, with an open, friendly face and dancing eyes. A good athlete and an above-average student, she was well liked at school. On December 6, 1941, she celebrated her fourteenth birthday. She was happy, confident, and secure.

And then, within twenty-four hours, the peace and comfort of her life were shattered.

• • •

On the morning of December 7, 1941, Japanese warplanes attacked Pearl Harbor. Home of a U.S. naval base, Pearl Harbor is located on the Hawaiian island of Oahu. Within two hours, bombs had rained down on every warship there. Nearby U.S. airfields were also bombed. Nearly 2,500 Americans were killed.

The following day, at President Roosevelt's request, Congress declared war on Japan. Only one Congress member, Jeannette Rankin, voted against the war declaration.

Now people of the U.S. began to fear the Japanese living among them. To many, it did not matter whether or not these Japanese were American citizens. They saw anyone of Japanese descent as the enemy. Some people wanted to imprison them all.

In the U.S. Territory of Hawaii, such an idea could not be carried out. There were 423,330 people living in Hawaii. Of these, 157,905 were of Japanese descent. That was too many people to put in jail. But their leaders could be got out of the way. The leaders began to be rounded up.

Japanese Buddhist and Shinto priests were arrested. So were teachers from Japanese language schools. Those schools—which many children, including Eugene and Patsy, attended daily for an hour after regular school— were shut down. Japanese newspapers also closed down, as their editors were taken away. Many of the people who were arrested were sent to prison camps on the U.S. mainland.

Anyone who was looked up to in the Japanese community was seen as a threat. Patsy's father was such a person. One night, two men came to the house and took him away in a car. "We have a few questions to ask you, Mr. Takemoto," was all that was said. Suematsu Takemoto said firmly to his family, "Don't worry. No one will harm me. I have committed no illegal act."

But there was no evidence that *other* people who had

been arrested had done anything illegal. They had not even been charged with a crime. Yet many of them had never returned to their homes.

Patsy, Eugene, and Mitama Takemoto did not sleep that night. Years later, Patsy Mink recounted:

> My father was questioned and allowed to return home to us. But we were fearful. We were under severe surveillance. Family friends were being arrested daily and hauled off to jail. I heard whispers about people being sent far away to prisons on the mainland. People started calling us vile names. My parents were greatly concerned about our safety.
>
> This experience was an important part of my development. It made me realize that one could not take citizenship and the promise of the U.S. Constitution for granted. I realized that everyone was terrified that they could be arrested for no reason at all, except that we were Japanese, like the enemy.

And the woman whose childhood had been lived in "Paradise" recalled: "I went to bed in the dark at night wondering if when I woke up in the morning, my dad would be gone."

CHAPTER 2

War and Peace

For many weeks after the bombing of Pearl Harbor, the public schools had been closed. Not until air raid trenches had been dug around the schools did they re-open. The older school children, including Eugene and Patsy, helped dig the trenches.

Even now, school was held only four days a week. The fifth day was given to "war duty," as it was called. Although girls had dug trenches alongside the boys, they were now given lighter work. Patsy reported for weekly duty with the Red Cross, to knit for the military. Eugene, on the other hand, reported to the cane fields. He and other boys helped with the plantation work. Their labor replaced that of men who'd gone to the armed forces.

Mr. and Mrs. Takemoto's families had escaped plantation labor years before. Now their son was working as a field hand. Some people might feel angry and bitter at such a turn of events.

But Mitama and Suematsu Takemoto didn't see things that way. They were very proud of both Eugene and Patsy's "war work." Like most Japanese-Americans, the Takemoto parents were eager to show that they were loyal to the U.S. government. Like the others, they felt grief and shame that anyone could believe they sided with Japan.

It was a troubled time for nearly everyone Patsy cared about. Yet, for Patsy, it was also a time of growth. Her life went on unfolding like a sturdy green leaf. She was building a foundation for the strong, capable adult she would become.

Very important to Patsy's growth at this time were her teachers. "I worshipped the ground on which they stood," she said of them. "I ate up everything they taught me." These *haole* teachers encouraged her to do her best. They expected her to make top grades; they expected her to go to college. Since childhood, Patsy had said she was going to become a medical doctor. Her teachers didn't voice any doubts that she would succeed.

Most important of all, perhaps, was the Maui High School principal.

He helped me a great deal during those terrible years—you know, the teens, when you're still struggling to find out who you are. He helped me by focusing my doubts and concerns into constructive activities, for the school.

He played a very significant role in my development—my self-confidence as a person. It made no difference to him that I was a girl student. He never indicated the slightest preference, in deciding various tasks—that it had to be given to a male or that it couldn't be done by a female. I think it was a mark of exceptional ability on his part to rise above the normal stereotypes of the day.

So, I did things like running for student-body president.

It was 1943 when Patsy decided to run for student-body president. Everyday life was somewhat better by then. Wartime tensions in Hawaii had eased a little. Some restrictions against Japanese-Americans had been lifted. Of greatest importance to them was that they were now accepted into the armed forces.

When the U.S. military called for Japanese-American volunteers, in 1943, they rushed to answer. Through no fault of their own, Japanese-Americans had been made to feel that they were the enemy. The sight of Japanese in the American uniform, they hoped, would erase their dishonor. The men who volunteered included those born in Japan, called *Issei*. The *Nisei*, or those who were American-born, volunteered by the thousands.

Patsy's father was among the Nisei who volunteered. He was forty-three, far past the age for military duties. He was turned down. But younger Nisei—nearly ten thousand of them from Hawaii—were taken into the U.S. Army. In the course of World War II, they were to become famous for their bravery in combat.

As these young people marched off to war, their country was badly mistreating the families they left behind. On the mainland U.S., 120,000 Japanese—over two-thirds of them American citizens—had been put into prison camps. Encircled by barbed wire fences, they lived in dreary, crowded, unhealthy surroundings. Most of them had lost everything they owned. The government had given them less than a week's notice to get ready to leave their homes. In that time, they had to sell whatever they owned. Their houses, furniture, businesses, and farms were snatched up by greedy buyers, for much less than their worth. Everything they'd gained from a lifetime of hard work was gone—overnight.

The U.S. government acted illegally, taking away the rights of its Japanese people. These people hadn't committed any crime. They were punished just because they were Japanese.

In Hawaii, the Japanese did not suffer the same kind of fate. In all, 1,500 were imprisoned. The Japanese people of Hawaii were not as free as they had been before the war. But their lives were still fairly normal.

Patsy's life in high school was normal, too. She continued to do well in school. It wasn't hard for her, because she liked studying and learning. Just for the fun of it, she took extra classes. Among these were debate and public speaking. She won second place for her school in a public speaking contest with other Hawaii schools. She also liked to organize events for her school, such as plays and picnics. It took time and effort, but the results were worth it.

It was school spirit that led her to run for student-body president. That, and the principal's belief in her. She put together a campaign team that was full of ideas and energy. The team worked hard to win the support of the students. When Patsy won, her team members were joyful.

Patsy didn't think of this as "my first political campaign." She didn't expect to go into politics. She had never even met anybody in politics. She expected to practice medicine. The Takemoto family doctor was one of her heroes. She hoped some day to have the kind of skills he had for helping people.

She didn't think of herself, either, as the first female student-body president of her high school. She *was* the first, but it wasn't talked about in her campaign. It didn't seem important to her team, or to Patsy. At the time, it wasn't her sex that seemed to matter to the world. It was her race.

At Maui High School, however, Patsy's race was not a drawback. Patsy knew that, in general, white people ran the Hawaiian Islands. But at Maui High School two-thirds of the student body was Japanese-American. Only ten percent was white. The white students didn't run the school. Patsy had only one white girlfriend who, like herself, was important in school affairs.

Her senior year flew by. It was busy and full, even though there were not many social events. Patsy says, "I enjoyed club activity. The best fun were things like selling candy at the football games." Neither Patsy nor her girlfriends dated. But by 1943, there were school dances on Saturday afternoons. U.S. Marines from nearby camps, invited by school officials, often came to the dances.

Except for the military, most people did not travel around on the island. No one was allowed to have much gasoline, because of the war. Patsy's family no longer attended their own church; it was too far away.

Patsy was sixteen when she graduated from Maui High School. Because she had the highest grades, she was named valedictorian of the class of 1944. Her parents gave her a graduation party, "the most memorable I ever had." It was a bittersweet occasion. Many of the boys in her class were headed off to war. She thought that some might not come back. And many did not.

Patsy herself was heading for the University of Hawaii, in Honolulu. She left in September. By the next year, when she was a sophomore, her parents had followed. Her father wanted to leave his job, to start his own business. Eugene was in the Army. Apart from some of Mitama's family living on Maui, there wasn't much to keep the Takemoto parents there.

In 1945, the war ended. Germany's defeat came first, in May. Japan surrended August 14. That was after U.S. planes dropped atomic bombs on two cities in Japan: Hiroshima and Nagasaki.

Like most Americans, the Takemotos knew very little about the terrible effects of the atomic bombs on human beings. Like others, they did not learn much until years later. They were simply glad that Germany and Japan had been defeated.

Suddenly, the whole world seemed to be in a new mood. Everyone seemed to be getting into motion. Japanese-Americans were free to travel anywhere now. Patsy got into motion, too. She decided to transfer to a college on the U.S. mainland.

She was sorry about her decision almost at once. She began her junior year at Wilson College, in Pennsylvania. She was very homesick. When winter came, it was a shock. The cold made her miserable. Worst of all, the college did not have what she wanted. She could not prepare there to enter medical school.

Patsy had some friends who were in medical school at the University of Nebraska. They suggested that she finish her junior year there. It might help her get into Nebraska's medical school. In January 1947, she transferred to the University of Nebraska, in Lincoln.

In Lincoln, another shock was waiting for her.

Patsy was given a room at the university's International House. That seemed fine to her, at first. It was a very nice place. But she soon found out something that was not at all nice. This was, that International House was there for only one purpose. It was there for "colored people." They were not allowed to live in any other dormitories.

When Patsy discovered this, she became furious. She wrote a letter of protest and mailed it to the local newspaper.

Then things began to happen:

I became an instant campus celebrity. Many students joined in this protest. Fraternities and sororities voiced their objection to the segregation policy. I was elected President of the Unaffiliated Student Association after only four months on campus.

Patsy Takemoto had taken an important political step. At the time, she did not know it. She did not think of writing a letter as "political." She did not know that other people would join her. She only knew she had to take a stand against this injustice.

In the future, she would sometimes succeed in such stands, sometimes not. This time, she did. That summer, the university changed its policy. From then on, all the dormitories were open to all races. It was a victory for equality.

But Patsy was not there to celebrate it. She was in Honolulu, and very ill. She never returned as a student to the school where she left a lasting mark.

CHAPTER 3

New Dreams for Old

Waking up in her hospital bed, the first thing Patsy saw were palm trees. Through the open windows she saw just the tops, brushing a blue sky. "It's Hawaii," she thought. "Home. . . ."

She turned her head. On one side of her bed was her father. On the other side, her mother stood. They were both smiling. Her father's smile was anxious.

"Feeling a little dizzy?" he asked. He added quickly, "You don't have to talk. Not unless you want to."

"I feel fine, Dad," said Patsy.

"Of course you're fine!" Mrs. Takemoto said. "Didn't the doctor tell us you'd be fine? Your father is such a worrier!"

Patsy saw that her mother's face looked tired and pale. Her mother had been worried, too. She just would not admit it. One of her mother's favorite sayings was: "Where's your *backbone*?"

Patsy had started to feel ill during the summer. That was when she'd gone home to her parents. Tests showed that she had thyroid trouble. It was a problem that could usually be cured by an operation. In mid-summer, she entered a Honolulu hospital.

Now the surgery had been done. Patsy felt relieved that the worst was over. Mainly, she was happy that the strain had been lifted from her parents. In a month or so, the surgeon had said, Patsy would be "as good as new." She could return to school.

It would cost too much money to return to Nebraska, however. She now planned to go to the University of Hawaii, for her senior year. And then what? Patsy's didn't know. Her shining hopes of getting into medical school were dimmer now. Still, she was not ready to give up.

Not yet.

• • •

Patsy stood on the porch of her parents' house, holding the letter in her hand. She slipped off her shoes before entering the house. (It is Japanese custom to remove shoes at the door.) Piling her books on a table, she stared at the envelope. Its return address was a U.S. mainland university.

Patsy didn't want to open the letter. Although the day was warm, and the room was sunny, she shivered.

At last, she tore open the envelope. Quickly, she scanned the letter. "We regret . . . at this time we are unable. . . . "

Patsy read the letter through. Then she read it again. She re-folded it and returned it to the envelope.

She sat down on the couch. Tears came to her eyes, but she brushed them away. It wasn't a time to cry, she thought. It was a time to think. A time to face facts.

Since her junior year at Nebraska, she had applied to over a dozen medical schools. Every one of them had turned her down. In a few months' time, she would graduate from the University of Hawaii. And she wasn't any closer to her goal. "This can't go on," Patsy thought.

It was hard to face defeat. But almost as hard to face was the question: *Why?* Why had she been rejected?

Patsy did not know, at the time, that medical schools admitted very few women. Furthermore, a record number of men were now applying to medical schools. Veterans of World War II, whose schooling was paid for by the government, had swelled the numbers. Against these odds, women had less chance than ever.

I had not thought that the reason I was rejected was because I was female. That thought did not come to me until much later. I thought that I was refused entry because I was not good enough, or possibly because I was Japanese. Anti-Japanese feelings were still quite high.

Whatever the reason, the facts could no longer be avoided. "I gave up all hope," she says, "of pursuing my lifelong dream."

Yet another kind of hope stayed with her. She had always felt that "one had to find a reason for one's existence. It seemed to me that possibly the highest achievement is to find a place in life that permits one to be of service to people." There was more than one path to such a goal, she knew.

By the following fall, Patsy was at the University of Chicago. She was admitted to its law school in 1948. There she set out on a new path, to pursue new dreams.

As with medical schools, not many women got into law schools in those days. Their chances were nearly zero at the best schools, like the University of Chicago. As a matter of fact, Patsy had been admitted by error. The law school had a quota for foreign students. And, Patsy explains, "Some idiot there thought Hawaii was a foreign country."

• • •

No two landscapes look less alike than Hawaii and the campus of the University of Chicago. Hawaii is all bright color. The University of Chicago is mostly grey. Stepping onto the campus, Patsy could believe she'd stumbled into Europe in the Middle Ages. She was surrounded by tall buildings made of matching brick. There were towers, arched windows, and pointed roofs with spires. Fantastic stone beasts peeped out from every nook.

Patsy lived on the campus in one of these buildings. Once again, she was at an International House. This one was truly international. Its purpose was not to separate non-white students from whites. The students who lived there came from many nations besides the U.S. As in Hawaii, there was a mix of languages, colors, and races. Patsy felt comfortable there.

But she seldom felt comfortable anywhere else. "It was a very dreadful first year," she says. "I don't remember really enjoying myself at all. It was so strange."

By her second year, she felt more at ease. She had learned to dress for the cold—more or less. The icy blasts from Lake Michigan stunned her, no matter how warmly she wrapped up. But she was beginning to enjoy herself. She began to understand why Chicago was known as a great university. Never before had she felt so challenged as a student. She had to work very hard.

She was surrounded by other students with good minds. Serious thinking did not end when a class period was over. There was interesting talk going on everywhere on the campus, all the time. It was an exciting place for someone like Patsy.

She soon had a circle of companions. Patsy did not need to work hard to attract people. They were drawn by her bright mind, her liveliness, her good looks.

"People just simply looked at her and wanted to be with her. She was obviously the leader in every respect." This was said by John Mink, a student and, later, Patsy's husband.

Patsy's studies and part-time jobs took up most of her time. There wasn't much left over for relaxing. She played cards, usually bridge, at International House, in the evenings after dinner. She wasn't a champion bridge player, but she enjoyed the game.

She was playing bridge the night she met John Francis Mink. "John, we need a fourth," someone at her table called out. A slim young man, reading in a nearby chair, raised his head. "Sure thing," he called back, and joined the table.

John Mink was studying geology at the University of Chicago. He came from Pennsylvania, and was a veteran of the recent war. An air force navigator, he had won many medals. He still wore a short military haircut. He was handsome, with blue eyes and a sparkling smile.

John and Patsy both called their first meeting "love at first sight." After that meeting, they could usually be seen at the same bridge table. Then, little by little, they spent less time with their bridge companions. They spent more and more time with each other.

They found a lot to talk about—their past lives, their plans for the future. They had in common a hope of helping to make a better world than the one they were living in. The end of World War II had not brought peace. Even now, the U.S. was at war again, in Korea. Within the U.S. itself, there were tensions, conflicts, and hatreds.

Race hatred was still one of the worst problems in the country. But for Patsy, this period was one of refuge from problems about her Japanese identity. She did not directly face anti-Japanese feelings on the campus or around Chicago. When she went with John to a restaurant or a movie, nobody stared. The sight of a white man and an Asian woman on a date didn't seem to startle anyone.

Perhaps Patsy and John might not have noticed, anyway. They weren't noticing much, now, except each other. Within six months of meeting across the bridge table, they decided to marry.

Patsy's parents were upset. They didn't want her to marry before she'd finished law school. Besides, they weren't sure it was a good thing for her to marry a *haole*, or white person. John's widowed mother wasn't so happy about the match, either. John admired his mother, and was devoted to her. She had supported him, his sisters and brothers after his father's death.

Patsy said later that "there did not seem at that point any way" to get the parents to approve. She and John didn't want to wait. "So we said, let's get married." Her face lights up with a smile. "And that's what we did."

Their wedding took place January 27, 1951, in the campus chapel. It was a simple wedding, and small, attended by student friends. The bride and groom were more dressed up than usual, but not in wedding clothes.

They found a small apartment to rent. It was clean, even if it was rather dark. They didn't spend much time in it. They were both usually on the campus. In June, both of them graduated. John received a master's degree in geology. Patsy was awarded her law degree.

She had already begun to make the rounds of Chicago law firms. She was eager to start work in her field.

But it seemed that no one was eager to employ her. She felt baffled. Times were good. John had found a job. Her law school classmates were finding jobs. Their records were no better than hers. "What's *wrong* with me?" she asked one of them, at last.

Her classmate looked amused. "Well," he said, "after all, Patsy, you're married. And your husband has a job."

"What's John got to do with it? We're talking about *me*."

He shook his head. "You don't find married women running around out there, Patsy."

"Out there? Out *where*?"

"On the job market. Usually, you find them at *home*."

Patsy became angry. Her classmate, she thought, was hiding something from her. But what was it? Was it because "white" firms didn't want to employ a Japanese-American?

She went on doggedly looking for a legal position. Meanwhile, she continued to work at the University of Chicago Law School library. Not until she was eight months pregnant did she leave that job.

Patsy and John were both very excited about the baby. It was a girl, born March 6, 1952. Her parents named her Gwendolyn Rachel Matsu Mink. Soon she became simply "Wendy."

Wendy didn't like the heat in Chicago any more than her mother liked the cold. "She was covered with prickly heat rash, from head to foot," Patsy recalls. As the summer went on, the heat got worse. At last, the discomfort became unbearable.

"So," Patsy says, "one day we said, 'This is it. We are not going to live here.' And we just packed our bags."

It was with six-month-old Wendy in her arms that Patsy Mink returned to Hawaii. A smiling John followed her into the balmy air of the Honolulu airport. She could see her parents waving.

"Home again!" thought Patsy gratefully. "This time, to *stay*."

But in this, she was mistaken. Patsy T. Mink still had a lot of traveling to do.

CHAPTER 4

In with Both Feet

Patsy sat at the desk in her tiny Honolulu office, staring at the phone. "Ring!" she commanded. But the phone didn't ring.

"Okay," Patsy said. "Okay, but you'd better ring soon." She made a face at the phone, and opened a book on her desk.

A year had gone by since the young Mink family had arrived in Honolulu. It had not taken long for Mr. and Mrs. Takemoto to become fond of John. And not surprisingly, they were delighted with their new grandchild. Wendy was by now toddling around their house, where both families lived.

John had quickly found a position as a geologist. Patsy, having passed the Hawaii bar examination, was licensed to practice law. She was the first Japanese-American woman lawyer in Hawaii history. Her family was very proud. Yet she soon found that no law firm wanted her.

It was like a dreadful re-play of her job search in Chicago. Except now she knew that her race wasn't the reason she was turned down. The Asian law firms were as unwilling to hire her as any others. Little by little, she understood why.

Sometimes the men who interviewed her said: "You're—well—*young* for a lawyer, Mrs. Mink." At twenty-six, Patsy knew she looked young. But she also knew that many of these men had begun working as lawyers at her age. No—age wasn't the problem.

Some of the men were more frank. They came right out and told her, "Law is a man's field. Our clients expect to be served by a man." Or they said, often looking bewildered: "But, Mrs. Mink, you're *married*!" A few even asked, "Why aren't you at home, taking care of your child?"

After a while, Patsy wanted to snap back, "Why don't you go home and take care of *yours*?" But she didn't, because it didn't sound polite. Her parents had taught her to be polite.

But her parents had taught her other things, too. They had taught her that, within reason, she could be whatever she wanted to be. A lawyer, they thought, was within reason. So when Patsy said, "Okay, I'll open my *own* law office!" they approved.

Mr. Takemoto knew that Patsy had no "paying customers." But he told her, "There's a small office for rent in my building. It would do as a law office. What if I pay the rent at first? When you have clients paying you, you can repay me." With a faint smile, he added, "The clients must not be too *big*. It's just a broom closet, that office."

Patsy laughed. "You really think I'll have clients, Dad?"

Her father said, with his usual firmness, "You will."

And a month later, here she was, in the "broom closet." She even had a few clients—although none had money for a fee. However, she now had a paid part-time job. She was teaching a business law class at the University of Hawaii. Her small paycheck took care of the rent for the office.

The telephone rang.

With the receiver at her ear, Patsy said, "Oh, Ken. How are you?" She hoped she didn't sound too disappointed. Ken was a friend, also just starting a law practice. *Not* a client. She listened, then said, "Yes, I guess I could. Yes, okay, I'll try. It sounds interesting. John may want to go, too."

Mr. Takemoto knocked at the door as Patsy put down the receiver. "Lunch?" he asked. Patsy laughed and held her palms up. "As you can see, I'm free." She glanced at her watch. "So long as I'm home when Mom gets Wendy up from her nap."

As they walked down the stairs to North King Street, Patsy said, "Ken Nakamura just phoned me. Do you remember him?"

Her father nodded. "A bright fellow. What's he up to?"

"Among other things, helping out the Democratic Party."

Mr. Takemoto looked surprised. Patsy said, "He asked if I'd go to a Democratic meeting tomorrow night. I think I will."

Mr. Takemoto looked even more surprised.

But he made no comment. He only asked Patsy where she'd like to have lunch.

• • •

Mr. Takemoto, who kept up with politics, did not take the Democratic Party of Hawaii seriously. Neither did most people in Hawaii.

Hawaii's economic life had long been controlled by

the big business firms that owned the plantations. These firms were known as "the Big Five." Their party was the Republican Party, which they also controlled.

Hawaii had become a U.S. territory in 1900. The Republican Party had been in power in Hawaii all the years since then. The governors of Hawaii, appointed by the U.S. President, were nearly always Republicans. And it was mostly Republicans who won election to Hawaii's territorial legislature.

But things were changing in Hawaii. The Big Five no longer ruled completely over Hawaii's economy. New industries had sprung up during the war, creating new jobs. The post-war boom in the tourist trade had also led to new jobs.

Most important of all was the growing power of the International Longshoremen's and Warehousemen's Union (ILWU). It had organized the sugar, pineapple, and waterfront workers. They now had better pay and working conditions.

There was a new spirit of hope among ordinary people. They wanted to have a say in running Hawaii. They wanted to make changes to help the mass of people in Hawaii. Therefore, they turned their attention to the Democratic Party.

In Hawaii, it was the Democratic Party that stood for ordinary people. But what good was that, thought the new-hopefuls, if the party always lost elections! It was time to make reforms in Hawaii's Democratic Party, they said. It was time for the islands' Democratic Party to stop being a joke.

On the telephone, Patsy's friend had briefly spoken about these ideas. He did not have to work hard to convince Patsy. She, too, wanted changes that would give more people a better life. Maybe working in a political party was a way to do that, she thought.

It was not by chance that the man who had phoned Patsy was a Japanese-American. For at the heart of the political reform movement were the Nisei veterans of World War II. Like their parents and grandparents, they had suffered from race hatred and suspicion. In the war, they had more than proved their patriotism. Their all-Nisei 100th Infantry Battalion, of the 442nd Regimental Combat Team, was the most highly decorated U.S. fighting unit. It also had the highest death rate. Now those who had survived wanted to take their places as first-class citizens of Hawaii. And at last they were in a position to do so, as Patsy later explained:

> The G.I. Bill [which paid educational expenses for veterans] was the real opening thrust for the local men. It was not only the war, coming back as heroes. It was the war *plus* the G.I. Bill, so that they could become doctors and architects and lawyers and whatever else—get their advanced degrees and come home and *be somebody*. That was really the breakthrough for the local Niseis who had participated in the war as members of the celebrated 442nd.

These young men did not want simply to rise, themselves. They wanted to lift the poor, the non-white, all who had been held down by the white ruling class. For this to happen, a lot of changes had to be made. The rich would have to pay more taxes. The poor had to have a better share of the land. Ordinary people had to have a chance in business, politics, and government.

The returning veterans also wanted improvements in public education. The G.I. Bill had given them *their* start.

They wanted to bring educational opportunities to others, too.

The young men believed that the key to such changes lay in politics. Japanese-Americans hadn't had much to do with politics before World War II. In Hawaii, the veterans changed all that. In doing so, they brought new life to Hawaii politics.

As for young Mrs. Mink, she leaped into the new political scene with both feet. "I got started in political activity in September of '53 when I went to my first political meeting," she says. "That was the beginning of everything."

Patsy was a newcomer, but so were almost all the others who wanted reform in the Democratic Party. The two "oldest" reformers were a one-armed veteran of the 442nd, Daniel Inouye, and an Irish Catholic ex-cop, John Burns. Together, they had organized the others. Both later reached high office.

Almost at once, Patsy began to have an effect on the scene.

I got involved and said, "Look, we've got to get more young people into the party. That's the only way we're going to revitalize it. We can't just use the old-timers who have been hanging around the party and losing every election. Not if we really want to develop new socio-economic policies for the Territory of Hawaii." So, that's how I got into Young Democrats' activities.

There was no branch of the Young Democrats in Hawaii. By the following summer, Patsy had succeeded in putting together the Oahu Young Democrats. Then she organized the Hawaii Young Democrats, throughout the islands. She was also working hard in the Democratic campaigns for the 1954 elections.

It was in 1954 that the Democrats won their first huge victory in Hawaii's territorial legislature. This victory is sometimes called, in Hawaii, the "bloodless revolution." It led to sweeping social welfare benefits, as the Democrats had promised. Yet their revolution could not be completed until Hawaii became a state. Until that happened, the people of Hawaii didn't have the right to elect their own representatives to the U.S. Congress. They didn't even have the right to elect their own governor. And in 1954, no one was sure when—or if—Hawaii would become a state.

Meanwhile, Patsy Mink had learned a lot about political campaigns. She began to ask herself: why shouldn't *she* run for office? True, she was busier, with new, paying clients. On the other hand, she wasn't as busy with Wendy, now in pre-school. What made up her mind, finally, was John Mink's urging her. "The next election has your name on it!" John said. When he offered to manage her campaign, Patsy said: "Okay. Let's go!"

On November 7, 1956, Patsy's name broke into Hawaii headlines. A typical one said: "Mrs. Mink Is First Nisei Woman To Become Territorial Legislator." She had easily won a seat in the House. Her well-managed campaign was called "level-headed" and "thoughtful." She was also called outspoken and independent.

Patsy went on being outspoken and independent after she took office. Around that time, the British had planned an atomic weapons test near Hawaii. Patsy's very first act was to ask the House to make an official protest. Her stand was one that many people didn't agree with. They wanted the U.S. and Britain to be ahead of the Soviet Union in the atomic weapons race. Those who were against testing atomic weapons were often smeared as "unpatriotic" or "communist."

Sure enough, a radio commenter called Patsy Mink a "communist pinko" because of her protest. Yet the House joined her protest without a single "nay" vote.

After that, Patsy had one success after another. She earned a name for hard work and sound thinking. She easily won election to the territorial Senate, in 1958. Once again, John managed her campaign. He was to manage all of them, in spite of the demands of his own career.

Patsy also went from one success to another in the Young Democrats of America. At its 1957 meeting in Reno, Nevada, she was elected vice-president of the organization. This position added to her experience. She made speeches around the U.S. and met national political leaders. Her interest in national politics was sharpened.

At home, excitement about Hawaii statehood grew every day. It had reached fever pitch by the time Patsy took her Senate seat. "No taxation without representation!" was one battle cry. More important was the feeling among the people of Hawaii that, "we're tired of being second-class citizens of the U.S." In fact, racism had played a part in delaying statehood. Many in the U.S. Congress didn't want to bring in a new state full of non-white peoples.

But now the drive for statehood couldn't be stopped. On March 12, 1959, Hawaii was at last admitted to the union.

Now Patsy and the other legislators were out of their jobs. New elections had to be held for a state legislature to replace the territorial one. And Hawaii also had to elect its very first representatives to the U.S. House and Senate.

"And so," relates Patsy Mink, "within a matter of weeks, I had to decide what to do. I decided to run for Congress. It was all very quick."

At first, it looked as though her election might also be very quick. When she filed for the single U.S. House seat allotted Hawaii, no Democrat opposed her. That gave her a straight shot to the general election. But she didn't stay unopposed.

Daniel Inouye, who had planned to run for the U.S. Senate, changed his mind at the last minute. He ran, instead, for the U.S. House. War-hero Inouye beat Patsy Mink, and went on to win the general election, too.

How did Patsy feel? "Oh, I was terribly discouraged!" she cries. "In fact, I swore I would never run again."

She bursts into laughter.

"Everyone, including my family, knew better!"

CHAPTER 5

The Eyes of the Doll

After Inouye defeated her, Patsy felt down. But she wasn't *out*. She wasn't out of a job. She went on with her law practice and her teaching. She wasn't even out of politics. She was still an active member of the Democratic Party.

In July 1960, a year after her defeat, Patsy went to Los Angeles. The Democratic Party was holding its national convention there. It was to decide on its platform and choose its candidate for U.S. President. Patsy went to the convention as a member of the Hawaii delegation. She favored Adlai Stevenson for the presidency.

Patsy was known to Democratic leaders because of her work in the Young Democrats of America. It was she who was chosen by the platform committee to give the speech for the civil rights plank. A noisy crowd of 10,000 was gathered at the blue and silver L.A. Sports Arena. Dressed in white, Patsy took her place before them. Five feet and one inch tall, she barely reached the microphones. But her voice rang out strongly. The crowd had grown very quiet by the time she neared the end of her speech.

> **If to believe in freedom and equality is to be a radical, then I am a radical. So long as there remain groups of our fellow Americans who are denied**

equal opportunity and equal protection under the law...we must remain steadfast, till all shades of man may stand side by side in dignity and self-respect to truly enjoy the fruits of this great land.

As Patsy finished her speech, the crowd was cheering. People pushed forward to shake her hand. The convention adopted the civil rights plank. Its promises to people of color went far beyond what some delegates wanted. Its stated aim was to guarantee, by law, equal access to "voting booths, schoolrooms, jobs, housing and public facilities." Most delegates from the South had strong objections. Patsy's forceful speech was given much credit for the victory of the civil rights plank.

The convention chose John Fitzgerald Kennedy as its nominee for President. Adlai Stevenson was not picked as the nominee for Vice-President. Instead, Kennedy chose Lyndon B. Johnson as his running mate.

No one could foresee that Kennedy, although elected to the presidency, would not live to serve out his first term. On November 22, 1963, he was killed by an assassin. Vice-President Lyndon Johnson was sworn in as President the same day.

At the moment, heading home from the 1960 convention, Patsy Mink was in high spirits. It had been exciting—not only being present at the convention, but taking part. The national political scene attracted Patsy. She wasn't at all frightened at the idea of being in the U.S. Congress. Still, she didn't feel ready to run for Congress again, such a short time after her defeat.

So, in 1962, she returned to Hawaii state politics. She ran for the state Senate—and won, by a very large margin.

Earlier, in the territorial Senate, Patsy had chaired the

Education Committee. She now got that position again and worked hard at it. She fought for money to improve Hawaii's schools. Winning a number of these battles, she became known as a champion of education. It was natural, then, that she had strong political support among people who wanted to improve education.

She made education the theme of her campaign when she ran for Congress again, in 1964. "I campaigned for federal aid to education very heavily," she recalls. "People thought I was stark raving mad. They'd taken polls which showed that no one was interested in education. It was a non-glamour issue."

I was scarcely mentioned in the papers at all as a candidate. They would have big stories about rallies. They'd write about the other two Democratic candidates. And I'd get maybe the last line in the column, which said, "And Patsy Mink was also at the rally." No one had the slightest belief that I had a prayer of winning.

When she did win the primary, Patsy says, some people were "in a state of shock." Among them were the leaders of Hawaii's Democratic Party. They had not supported her; in fact, they had quietly worked against her. This wasn't because her public positions weren't the same as those of the Democrats. Her positions, so far, had been mainly the same.

What the Democratic leaders didn't like was that Patsy T. Mink went her own way. They couldn't control her. She never checked with the party on what to do or say. She felt strongly that "no one was going to tell me what to do." As a result, many party Democrats supported her Republican opponent when the general election came.

The people working in Patsy's campaign were loyal, but their number was small. Her campaign fund was small, too. It came mostly from little gifts of no more than $25. The big money went to the Republican candidate. With all those things against her, once again nearly everyone expected Patsy to lose. But John and Patsy never stopped aiming for victory and never lost hope.

At the beginning of the campaign, Patsy had bought a Japanese *daruma* doll. The eyes of the doll are blank. By an old custom, one eye of the doll is painted in for a new wish. The other eye is painted in when the owner's wish comes true. Patsy carefully painted in one eye.

On the day after the election, Patsy painted in the *daruma* doll's missing eye. The voters had made their surprising choice. For the first time in history, an Asian-American woman had been elected to Congress.

That was exactly where Patsy Mink wished to be.

• • •

John Mink was happy to go to Washington, D.C., with Patsy—and able to. His successful career as a geologist gave him a lot of choices of jobs. He resigned his Honolulu position for one at a university in the Washington, D.C. area.

Twelve-year-old Wendy wasn't upset by the sudden move from home, as many her age might be. Outgoing and confident, she looked forward to new experiences. She had never seen snow!

Every member of the family felt eager to begin life in the capital. Still, it wasn't easy to get settled 5,000 miles from home. As Patsy later recalled, "It was all very new, and so different."

Everything needed to be done at once. I had to get my office furniture in, and hire a staff. I had to find out where things were and who people were that had responsibility for different things. In addition to that, we had to find a place to live and get our daughter enrolled in a school.

Members of the House of Representatives are elected to two-year terms. Then, if they want to stay in office, they have to run again. They can't be sure they'll be re-elected. All the stress of settling may be for the sake of a rather short stay.

For Patsy, the stress was lightened by John's help. They have always been equal partners in their marriage, sharing childcare and domestic tasks. Their household is organized to benefit both of them. "It is not the purpose of our living to make our marriage work," Patsy says. "The purpose is to do things you want to do."

John Mink takes a strong interest in politics—and in Patsy. Patsy's political career brings these two interests together. By choice, he is the only person who has ever served as her campaign manager. Patsy thinks that this is "ideal."

I wouldn't have it any other way, frankly. To be able to air real deep worries in an open and frank kind of a way with someone who actually can do something about it, as your campaign person, is great. Talking to just another person who isn't involved in the campaign and can't take charge is not as helpful. And, no matter how close you are with a staffer, I'm always reluctant to let it all hang out, in terms of my feelings. . . . You can't really express yourself in the way you are able to do with your husband.

Besides being her campaign manager, John is Patsy's main "sounding board," she says. He is her "in-house critic," with whom she debates her views.

Patsy thinks that a good many Congresswomen have this "ideal" arrangement. Even if the husbands aren't campaign managers, they are "extremely involved." It would be surprising if it were not so. At the very least, a Congresswoman's husband who takes no share of domestic cares is probably rare. A woman with a demanding public life can't carry the whole burden of home life—any more than a man can.

For many people, the idea of a woman in public life was still hard to accept when Patsy went to Congress in 1965. Nearly half a century had gone by since the first woman, Jeannette Rankin, had entered Congress. You would not have known it from the news stories about Patsy. Most of them dwelt on the fact that she was a woman. They said little about her public career.

"Do you think it's a disadvantage for a woman in politics to be pretty?" the *Honolulu Advertiser* asked Patsy. The new U.S. Representative merely said, "I don't think it's a disadvantage." Not content with this brief reply, the interviewer continued along the same lines. Rep. Mink was "pretty, articulate, informed, able, and of Japanese ancestry." Did she therefore expect that she "might arouse considerable attention" in Washington, D.C.? Patsy answered, "Yes"—then pointed out, "There's a lot of work and that's what I'll expect to be doing."

She was not asked for her plans for getting more federal aid to education. Instead, she was asked if she planned "to buy a new wardrobe." (Daniel Inouye, when first elected to Congress, was not asked what he planned to wear in the Capitol.)

The article dwelt upon women's supposed habit of crying a lot. Was it fair, the *Advertiser* asked Rep. Mink, for "lady politicians" to shed tears to get their way? She answered that she had never cried during a session of the State Legislature. She added that she had not seen other female legislators weep. The *Advertiser* then went on to quote other Hawaii politicians who had "seen plenty of lady legislators weep."

Some offered reasons the poor ladies might burst into tears. The mayor of Honolulu said that women in politics often "don't understand" the business side of government. But his opinion of Rep. Mink didn't quite fit that sweet, helpless picture. "The Washington crowd will have its eyes opened when Patsy starts operating," he said. "She has the qualities of a tiger."

Member of Congress or not, Patsy was a woman. In the eyes of society, that meant she had to be classed as either a kitten or a tiger. Patsy Takemoto Mink was neither one. Like other women, she was a person. Of course, she was also an unusual person—and an unusual woman. If not, she would not have been on her way to Congress.

The number of women in Congress at any one time had never reached more than twenty. In 1965, when Patsy took her seat, there were only twelve—out of a total of 535 members. It took courage to face such odds. But there was something more remarkable. Patsy was also the first woman of color ever elected to Congress.

Four years later, Shirley Chisholm was the first black woman to win a seat in Congress. That was seen as the very great event that it was. Yet it was Patsy who led the way. This fact is rarely mentioned by anyone, starting with Patsy. Interviewed by *Life* on the eve of her first term in Congress, she said:

I feel, act and live like any other American the country over. What I bring to Congress is a Hawaiian background of tolerance and equality that can contribute a great deal to better understanding between races.

It was a mild statement, almost sunny. Nothing in it foretold the battles for equal justice Patsy Mink was to wage over the coming years in Congress.

CHAPTER   6

Troubled Times

Patsy T. Mink was sworn into the U.S. House of Representatives on January 4, 1965. Re-elected five times, she went on to serve an unbroken twelve years, to 1977.

That period of twelve years was one of the most explosive in the nation's history. During those years there was upheaval on college and high school campuses. There were hard-won victories as well as tragedy in the black civil rights movement. The years saw the rise of a new women's movement. They also saw the "war on poverty," a giant effort by government to improve the lives of the country's poor. Above all, those were the years of deep conflict over the Vietnam War.

It was almost impossible for anyone who lived in the U.S. to be untouched by one or more of these events. For a member of Congress, it wasn't possible at all.

A member of Congress, sooner or later, had to decide what to say about these events. Sometimes he or she had to decide how to vote on laws connected with them. That could be uncomfortable. People had strong feelings about what was going on in the country. Members of Congress could lose their popularity with voters by taking one stand or another. Or they might lose the support of those who gave money to their campaigns.

Some Congress members said and did whatever they thought would please the most supporters. Many tried to avoid taking a clear stand. They said first one thing, and then another.

That wasn't Patsy Mink's way. People always knew where she stood.

Rep. Mink made herself clear her very first day in Congress. She joined a small group of members in protesting the seating of the House members from Mississippi. The protesters wanted to show that they opposed Mississippi's election practices. Those practices cheated black Americans of their voting rights.

Few House members voted for the protest, so the Mississippi members were seated. But not long after, national leaders joined those who demanded changes in Mississippi's racist elections. The action of the protesters helped bring that about.

In Hawaii, most people favored the stand Patsy had taken. In the district Patsy represented, sixty-four percent of the population was non-white. It isn't surprising that most of the people liked her stand for racial equality.

They did not like all her views, however. She was opposed to U.S. military action in Vietnam. That wasn't a popular position in Hawaii. Many of the people in Patsy's district had jobs with the military. The war in Vietnam, creating even more such jobs, was believed to be good for the economy. Besides, people felt it wasn't patriotic to oppose U.S. military activity.

Patsy called the Vietnam War "a jungle of horrors." The U.S. had begun giving economic aid to South Vietnam as far back as 1954. The purpose of the U.S. was to oppose the Communist side, in the fight between North and South Vietnam. By 1964, U.S. troops were taking part in the actual fighting in Vietnam.

From Patsy's viewpoint, the U.S. had no right to interfere in Vietnam. She said it was wrong to sacrifice young American lives in that far-off land. She also pointed to the billions of dollars spent to kill "poor and wretched" Asians. That money, she said, was needed at home—to help poor and wretched Americans.

Did Rep. Mink worry that her anti-war views might hurt her career? An interviewer asked her this question some years later. She answered that she "never gave it a thought."

It was a case of my living up to my own views and conscience. If I was defeated for it, that's the way it had to be. There was no way in which I could compromise.

When Patsy began speaking out on the war, she had almost no company in Congress. President Lyndon Johnson—like herself, a Democrat—was a "hawk," as those who favored the war were called. Her fellow-Hawaii Congress members—two Democrats, one Republican—supported the war. It wasn't until 1969 that the two Democrats flipped over to the same side as Patsy. They didn't start to oppose the war until a Republican President, Richard M. Nixon, was waging it.

Patsy admits "it was tough" to go against the majority. Luckily, she has what her mother called "backbone." The *Honolulu Star-Bulletin* once quoted her as saying:

It is easy enough to vote right and be consistently with the majority, but it is more often more important to be ahead of the majority. This means being

willing to cut the first furrow in the ground and stand alone for a while if necessary.

She faced another hard test in 1968, although this time it wasn't her burden alone. In the spring of that year, with others in the nation, she took two crushing blows. The Rev. Martin Luther King, Jr., and Sen. Robert F. Kennedy were assassinated within two months of each other. Patsy had looked to their leadership for a just and peaceful world. With their deaths, she felt "a good part of my life seemed to wither away also."

Yet, after a time, a new resolve rose in her. A citizen in a democracy ought not to depend so heavily on great leaders, she thought. With King and Kennedy gone, she felt she needed to speak out even more strongly for beliefs she shared with them. She would continue to work for peace and for what she called "simple justice and equality."

• • •

Patsy's two-room suite in the Longworth House Office Building was larger than her first law office in Honolulu. But it was still quite small. The eight members of her staff could just squeeze into the outer room. However, when all of them were at their desks, there was no place for a visitor to sit down.

In Patsy's inner office were a desk, a desk chair, a bookcase, and a couch. Helen Lewis, Patsy's office manager, sometimes jammed in a second chair.

Helen Lewis laid out Patsy's mail on the desk daily. One morning in 1967, Patsy's eye fell on a House bulletin among the letters. It was a notice of an exercise class, "for members only." Something about it nagged at Patsy, but she put it aside.

A while later, her phone rang. As she listened to a musical female voice, her eyes began to sparkle. "Yes," she said. "Sure, okay. When?" She picked up the House bulletin, quickly scanning it. "With Catherine May? Terrific!" She giggled once, after she'd hung up. Then she went back to work.

In fact, the brief plans she'd made on the phone were also her work. The planning was for a light-hearted protest against a real problem. Two days later, the protest was headline news. There were front-page stories as far away as Paris, France.

The newspaper photo showed three women outside the door of a gym. A sign on the door said "Members Only." A young male guard blocked the doorway. He wore a sheepish grin. "It's just for members of Congress," he was quoted as saying. All three women were identified as members of the U.S. Congress. They were Catherine May, of Washington, Charlotte T. Reid, of Illinois, and Patsy T. Mink, of Hawaii.

True, the three women had been elected to Congress. The mostly male members of that body were keeping it a male club, all the same. The "reason" the men gave for barring female members from the gym was that "men liked to swim nude."

"So we said," Patsy reported later, "'Is it too much for the democratic process to ask you to put your pants on?'"

Catherine May and Charlotte Reid were both Republicans. Charlotte Reid was, besides, a fervent supporter of the Vietnam War. But Patsy was glad to join them both in a protest against sex discrimination. It wasn't the first time she'd joined lawmakers of different views, to work toward common goals. These efforts failed sometimes. (In this case, the Congressmen didn't open the gym to Congresswomen.) But sometimes they succeeded.

Patsy went to Congress at the start of President Lyndon B. Johnson's first full term of office. Johnson soon started a national campaign that became known as the "war on poverty." Between 1965 and 1967 alone, Congress enacted sixty-seven new programs meant to improve life for the poor. Patsy took an interest in all of them.

Some of her most intense efforts went to programs for schools. She kept her campaign promises to work for federal aid to education. She got onto the House Committee on Education. It was this committee that wrote the education bills for the House to consider. Patsy wrote bills to benefit needy youth, from pre-school to college. She argued for these bills with great success. She cared deeply about the welfare of the young.

The war on poverty went to the heart of another of Patsy's deepest concerns. That concern was for women living in poverty. The poverty programs gave these women a chance for jobs, education, health care, and other benefits. As Patsy said, poor women "had simply been left out of" such programs in the past. What social programs there were, before, had mostly served men. Yet many more women than men were in need:

Women are the ones that are the most severely damaged by poverty, whether it's as single heads of households or mothers of dependent children, or as

working women who belong to the very bottom of the wage scale. So women had a great stake in the success of the program.

An interviewer asked Patsy how she came to have these strong feelings about poor women. After all, Rep. Mink herself had never lived in poverty. Patsy said, "I don't know. I realized that my life was not typical of other women in the country." She went on to say:

> And because women were not in politics, and because there were only eight women at the time who were members of Congress, I felt I had to speak for them, because they didn't have people who could express their concerns. So, I always felt that we were serving a dual role in Congress, representing our own districts and, at the same time, having to voice the concerns of the *total* population of women in the country.

Patsy was not happy that most Congresswomen didn't share her views of their duty. "They *refused* to voice those concerns. So that made it even more difficult for myself and [Reps.] Edith Green, Martha Griffiths, Julia Hansen." Some women who later got to Congress also worked hard on women's issues. But their numbers remained small during the years of the poverty programs.

The poverty programs would later disappear, under Republican leadership. But even in the mid-sixties, they were in trouble. The war on poverty and the Vietnam War were on a collision course. This was so although the same man led them both.

That man was President Lyndon B. Johnson, known as "LBJ."

He was determined to turn the U.S. into what he called the "Great Society." By this, he meant a society freed of poverty, in which everyone had an equal chance. He went after this goal fast and effectively. Under his leadership, Congress voted more money for welfare programs than it had voted the entire twenty years before.

Congress also voted more and more money for the Vietnam War. LBJ believed that the U.S. could win the war fast. He was mistaken. But he wouldn't give up the Vietnam War *or* the war on poverty. He didn't want to trim a dime from either one.

Most members of Congress were willing to go along with the Vietnam War. But growing numbers of Americans were *not*. The war was costing too much money—with no end in sight. Too many American lives had been lost. Many people also objected to the wholesale killing and torture of Vietnamese by "our side." There was special horror at the murder and maiming of children.

Protest against the war grew daily. There were more, and larger, demonstrations. By 1968, the nation was in an uproar. There were marches, picket lines, sit-ins, strikes, and riots throughout the country. Wherever the President went, he was followed by what he called "that horrible song": *"Hey, hey, LBJ, how many kids did you kill today?"* President Johnson had dreamed of helping kids—not killing them.

At the end of March 1968, the President went on TV. He said that he had ordered a cutback in the bombing of Vietnam. He spoke of his plans for seeking peace. He then caused even more surprise among his listeners. He announced that he would not accept the nomination of his party for another term as President.

The President gave as his reason the country's deep

division about the Vietnam War. Those who opposed the war rejoiced at this. They had, at last, had a powerful effect. The President himself admitted that huge numbers did not support his Vietnam policy. They dared to hope that this was the beginning of the end of the war.

They were wrong. It was President Johnson's war on poverty that was beginning to end. The war in Vietnam was going to continue—and for a long, long time.

CHAPTER 7

The Company of Women

With a new President in office, the angry chant of *"Hey, hey, LBJ"* died away. But other chants still filled the air.

All we are saying is give peace a chance!

What do we want? Peace! When do we want it? Now!
Peace—now! PEACE—NOW, PEACE—NOW!
PEACE—NOW!

The new President, Richard M. Nixon, had said in his campaign that he had a "plan" for ending the Vietnam war. Some people voted for him because they believed what he said. He even got some Democratic votes that way, although he was a Republican.

But the war didn't end. In fact, President Nixon stepped up the bombing of Vietnam. He also began to bomb the nearby country of Cambodia. He kept some of these things secret. Yet people got enough information to know that the killing still went on. So the demonstrations didn't stop. There were more than ever.

Not all the demonstrations were about the war. There were public protests about the need for housing and schools, about the environment, about farmworkers' rights. There were ongoing demands for African-

American rights, American Indian rights, Chicano rights. But the fastest-growing demand of all was for women's rights.

A whole new movement had begun, spilling out onto the streets and sidewalks. It called itself the Women's Liberation Movement. Its purpose was to achieve rights and opportunities for women equal to those of men. One of the first targets of the movement was to get women a fair deal in employment.

Patsy Mink was there ahead of the new movement. In the Hawaii State Senate, she'd sponsored an equal-pay-for-equal-work bill. Its target was employers who didn't pay women fair wages. That was in 1962, before there was a women's liberation movement.

In Congress, Patsy kept up her efforts to advance women's rights. In 1970, her efforts created a storm. At that time, President Nixon had nominated a judge named G. Harrold Carswell to serve on the U.S. Supreme Court, Before a justice can be appointed to the Supreme Court, the Senate Judiciary Committee must give its approval. Rep. Mink went before that committee to ask that Carswell be turned down.

She angrily pointed to Carswell's record on women's rights. The record showed that Carswell had upheld an employer's right to deny a job to a woman because she had young children. Could a man be denied a job on the same grounds? The answer was no. Judge Carswell's ruling, said Rep. Mink, showed "a total lack of understanding of the concept of equality . . . and the right of women to be treated equally and fairly under the law."

No other member of Congress had made this complaint. Patsy's lone voice set off a rare chain of events. Both houses of the Hawaii State Legislature asked that

Carswell be turned down. Their grounds were the same as Patsy's. The Republican Senator from Hawaii had supported Carswell. Now he said he would vote against him. Nixon himself paused to reconsider. In the final vote of the Senate, Carswell was defeated.

Nobody had ever raised a women's rights issue against a Supreme Court nominee. Patsy had been "willing to cut the first furrow," for women. A longtime friend of hers remarked, "Patsy was a liberated woman long before the movement had a name."

Patsy had the company of a lot of strong-minded women by now, however. In 1966, the National Organization for Women (NOW) was founded. It started work on every issue that affected women. Women were carrying on struggles for equality in education and employment. They were struggling for childcare centers and welfare payments. They were fighting for the right to birth control and abortion. By the late 1960s, they could no longer be ignored or controlled. They couldn't be "kept in their place."

Of course, there were those who still thought they could—and should. Rep. Mink got into a big quarrel with one such person. His name was Dr. Edgar Berman. Like Patsy, he was a member of a Democratic Party planning committee that met in 1970. Patsy asked the committee to plan for including women in high public offices. She said she hoped that the day of a woman President was not far off.

Dr. Berman declared that this was a very foolish idea. He went on to lecture Patsy before the committee. He said that women had limits as leaders. This, said the doctor, was because of their physical make-up and menstrual cycle. Especially, he added, women in menopause could not be trusted as leaders. "Suppose," he said, "that we had a menopausal woman President." In a crisis, her mind would be at the mercy of her hormones. That would be dangerous for the fate of the nation.

Patsy was furious that a man with these backward ideas had been put on the committee. She fired off a letter demanding that he be removed. Dr. Berman showed "the basest sort of prejudice against women," Patsy wrote. She compared his mocking of women to the ideas of those who believed that black people weren't as good as white people.

Patsy's letter got a lot of publicity. The Democratic Party leaders couldn't ignore it. Neither could Dr. Berman. He stuck to his views about women—but he resigned from the committee.

Patsy's protest had been joined by others. Among them was Rep. Shirley Chisholm, a recently elected Democrat. This first African-American woman in Congress was never afraid to speak her mind. She observed that "one thing people are afraid of in Shirley Chisholm is *her mouth*." Newer still in Congress was Democratic Rep. Bella Abzug. Bella, as everyone called her, was also fearless. And Rep. Margaret Heckler, a Republican, spoke and voted as she pleased—often against her party.

Thus, in Congress, too, Patsy had the company of some strong-minded women. "Uppity women," many thought. Perhaps it might be expected that at least one of them would make a run for President. In 1971-72, two of them did. Those two were Shirley Chisholm and Patsy T. Mink.

Patsy did not suppose that she could become President. She ran in order to turn a spotlight on urgent issues. Highest on her list was Vietnam. She charged that President Nixon "lied in 1968 when he said he had a Peace Plan to end this miserable war." She attacked him for using "national security" as a shield to hide facts about the war. The President, she said, did not respect "the people's right to know." For that, he should be removed from office, Rep. Mink said.

Patsy gave another reason for running. That was to get the nation to face its sexist notions of women. Dr. Berman gave a crude picture of the real, hidden beliefs of many other people. Patsy believed that people must come to view a female President as *thinkable*. If not, "the concept of absolute equality" was simply pretense, said Rep. Mink.

Patsy also called for strong support for civil rights and for better social welfare programs. These were areas of public concern that had been weakened under Nixon. Impressed by Patsy, a group of liberal Democrats in Oregon asked her to be their presidential candidate in 1971. She accepted, and was on the ballot in Oregon's presidential primary, held in May 1972.

In April of that year, Patsy and Bella Abzug made a trip to Paris. That was where meetings were being held to try to settle the Vietnam conflict. There were representatives of North Vietnam and South Vietnam at the meetings. There were representatives of the Communist-led forces (Viet Cong) which opposed the South Vietnam government. And there were United States representatives. But the U.S. had broken off its part in the meetings. Now the peace talks were stalled.

No one knew why the U.S. had stopped talking in Paris. No one was told what was going on in Paris *or* in the war. Congress could not get any information from its own government. A number of Congress members, by now, were angry and upset. A stream of them had visited Paris. They didn't learn anything. Patsy and Bella decided to go on their own fact-finding mission. They wanted to question all parties involved in the conflict.

In Paris, they talked with representatives of each of the parties. They asked what efforts each side was making to re-start the talks, and what each saw as ways to achieve peace. They asked for information on all aspects of the war.

They made a special effort to meet a woman leader. She was Madame Ngyen The Binh, of the Viet Cong. With her they brought up some of the "human" issues. They asked about the Vietnamese-American orphans who were children of U.S. soldiers. Was there a way they could be allowed to immigrate to the U.S.? They tried to find out about the welfare of American prisoners of war.

What did they learn from the Paris trip? In Patsy's words:

Nothing. Nothing. Nothing. We found out absolutely nothing. It was a total bust! Our government in particular didn't want to tell us anything. The public again was being kept out of what was going on.

Asked if speaking with any of the other parties had any effect, Patsy answered: "No, no. I'm sure it had none at all."

She wouldn't make something out of nothing, wouldn't lie about it. She and Bella reported back to Congress. They could only admit that their mission had not moved peace forward. Upon her return, Patsy tried to move Congress forward. Speaking to the House, she called for an immediate end to the war. It was the sixth of similar attempts she'd made in a year. This time, more than half the House voted with her. But the war still went on.

Patsy had continued her efforts on other fronts. Back in 1967 she had written a bill to provide childcare for working mothers. In 1971, it at last seemed to be getting somewhere. It would provide health care and nutrition. Education, bilingual education, and special care for the disabled were other features. It had strong support from Republicans as well as Democrats.

But President Nixon vetoed the bill. In her Oregon Presidential campaign, Patsy spoke about this. She spoke of the small children left alone at home while both parents worked. Nixon, she said, had showed how little he cared about that.

Patsy's showing in the primary was only two percent of the vote. There were, however, nine others on the Democratic ballot. Patsy didn't regret time and energy given to the campaign. She had run as a protest against the war and to challenge ideas about women. She believed that she had made gains, especially for the idea of women as political leaders. "There'll be a woman Vice-President sooner than might otherwise have been the case," she said. Having done what she set out to do, she pulled out of the Presidential race.

Now it was time to run for an office she *did* intend to win. She was up for re-election to her House seat.

Patsy often went home to Hawaii. The flight from Washington took twelve and a half hours. It was worth the time, to Patsy. It meant direct touch with the people she represented.

In 1972, when she went home to campaign, she faced trouble. It came from the leaders of Hawaii's Democratic Party. They didn't approve of Patsy. She had recently attacked them for limiting women's power in party affairs. They chose a man named John Goemens to run against her in the Democratic primary election.

Goemens blasted Rep. Mink for her support of anti-war demonstrations. They were peaceful protests, but Goemens tried to link Patsy with anti-war riots. He also raged about her trip to the Paris peace talks. He accused her of being a traitor for talking with Communists there.

By now, this tactic was a common one. Anyone who worked for peace could be smeared as pro-Communist. Goemens believed this was an especially good tactic in Hawaii. Its economy depended a lot on the military.

The same tactic had been used against Patsy in the 1968 campaign. It backfired then. And it backfired now.

Newspapers soon noted the "shabby treatment" given Patsy by the Democratic leaders. The *Honolulu Star Bulletin* praised her for "making her positions known." A labor paper observed: "Among our Representatives, Mrs. Mink has had the most national exposure and has run up a consistently brilliant performance." The *Bulletin* wrote harshly of Goemans's "dirty" tactics. Senator Ted Kennedy, brother of slain President John F. Kennedy, sent Patsy a letter to be made public. The attacks on her patriotism were "outrageous," he wrote. "I hope that I can look forward to continuing to serve with you in the 93rd Congress."

In the primary, reports Patsy, she "wiped Goemens out and he was never able to run for office successfully again. The people in Hawaii do not like smear tactics." She went on to defeat her Republican challenger easily.

The Republicans ran a woman against her. This had been tried before, with no effect on voters. Patsy says, "There was a feeling that I was hard to beat if a male ran, but that a female might have a chance." She adds humorously: "I don't know why they thought that. I never really campaigned on being a woman, anyway. I've always assumed it was self-evident."

Being a woman hadn't been what counted, in her case. What counted was the quality of Patsy Mink.

CHAPTER 8

Backbone

Patsy's Washington office was small, but the desk was big. Behind it, the Representative from Hawaii looked especially tiny and delicate, and much younger than her age. Yet her voice didn't match the picture. It was a rich voice, mature and self-confident. A no-nonsense voice.

It was a voice that forced people to take Patsy seriously. "Petite and pretty" Patsy sometimes made people think of a cheerleader. That image is not helpful to a politician. Patsy overcame it by what she said, and also by how she said it. Her voice was loud and strong enough to carry without a microphone. In arguing, she jabbed the air with a finger, or pounded on a desk. So, when Patsy made a speech—as she often did—she didn't remind anybody of a cheerleader.

On a bright fall day in 1973, Patsy was preparing to give a speech in the House. Her dark head bent over the typed copy on her desk. She worked silently, adding a note here and there. Once in a while she raised her head, thinking. Her eyes fell on a framed snapshot of her father. In his arms were a black dog and a black cat.

Suematsu Takemoto loved animals, as Patsy did. She had happy memories of him playing with the family's many pets. And now her father was gone. He had died in

the midst of her last campaign, a year ago. She was still re-
covering from the blow. Even so, she drew strength from
thoughts of her much-loved "Dad." He'd had great faith
in her. Not just in her abilities, but in her "backbone."

She needed to remember that now. In her speech today, she planned to attack President Nixon. That was going to displease a lot of people. Well, then, thought Patsy,
that's how it had to be. The main thing was to try to stop
the harm the President was doing to the country.

For more than a year, President Nixon's office had
been soiled by scandal. People close to him had been accused, and found guilty, of many crimes. Nearly every
crime had to do with helping Nixon win the 1972 race for
President.

The first crime to come to light was a burglary of
Democratic Party headquarters. It took place in Washington, D.C., in the Watergate building. Its purpose seemed
to be to allow Republican Party workers to spy on the
Democrats. The break-in had been traced indirectly to a
person on the President's staff.

The President denied knowing anything about any of
this. At the same time, he tried to stop every attempt to investigate. It had begun to look very much as if the President were lying. Yet Congress hung back from taking any
strong action.

So Patsy planned to ask Congress to start a process to
accuse the President of wrong conduct in office. This
process—impeachment—could force into the open any
facts Nixon was hiding. It could very well lead to his re-
moval from office.

Now Rep. Mink gathered up her papers and left her
office. Heels tapping, she started along the many hallways
that led to the House chamber. Outside the chamber,

some young people recognized her. They knew her for her struggle against the war. "Hi, Patsy!" they shouted. One cried: "Sock it to 'em, Patsy!" Patsy's smile flashed at them as she entered the chamber. Inside, as she moved to her seat, she was greeted by House members. Some greetings were warm—a hug, a handshake, a pat on the back. Some were only polite—the bare flick of a smile, a quick nod. People tended either to adore Patsy or to find her upsetting. Her tongue could be very sharp.

It was sharp today when she stood to address the House. She spared no words as she accused the President of hiding key facts from the people.

He has stepped between the promised investigation and the right of Americans to know the final answer to the question of the President's conduct in office. He has broken the people's trust both in him and in the office of the Presidency. I regard this as a high crime against the people of this Nation.

Rep. Mink's eyes flashed. Her voice rose, filling the chamber. "This nation is in need of moral leadership. It obviously cannot expect it from the President. It must be able to expect it from the Congress.

"I believe," she concluded, "we must proceed with the impeachment of President Nixon so that the American people can finally know that justice has prevailed."

As Patsy sat down, her heart wasn't pounding. She was calm. She had not rushed into her decision to take this action. As usual, she had gone over everything with John Mink. That often had the effect of making her think twice.

She had thought long enough about this matter. She felt completely sure that she was doing the right thing.

Before Patsy made her speech, a number of citizens'

groups had already called for impeachment. The Senate was holding "Watergate" hearings, watched by millions on TV. More and more people began to join the cry for impeachment. It was high time for Congress to listen.

Four months after Patsy's speech, the House brought impeachment charges against the President. President Nixon didn't want to face a trial for impeachment. On August 8, 1974, he resigned.

Vice-President Gerald Ford now became President. Patsy knew Ford from her first days in Congress. He'd been a leading Republican member of the House at that time. Patsy had never felt toward him the deep dislike and distrust she felt toward Richard Nixon. However, one of Ford's first acts as President was to pardon Nixon for any crimes he may have committed. Patsy was very angry. She spoke out strongly against this new betrayal of justice.

Even so, she was happy to see the last of Nixon in the White House. On New Year's Eve, at home in Hawaii with her family, she greeted 1975 hopefully.

Nothing warned her that the coming year would bring the worst trial she had ever faced. So far, it was her political struggles that had tested Patsy's strong "backbone." This time, it was going to be her private life.

• • •

As 1975 began, Patsy had been a politician for more than twenty years. She had been a mother longer than that.

Wendy Mink was an only child. That wasn't a matter of chance. Patsy had been set on a career before Wendy's birth. She had remained set on it. That being so, she thought she could be a good mother to one child. But not more than one.

And she had done well, with John's help. All the same, it hadn't always been easy. Once, when Wendy was four, she helped her mother pass out campaign leaflets. The next day, the child came down with chicken pox. Patsy thought of the cases of chicken pox Wendy may have given out with the leaflets.

It wasn't really a joke. Sometimes, as on that day, good childcare wasn't to be had. When Patsy fought for bills for quality childcare, she knew the problems at first-hand.

On the whole, however, things had gone well for the Mink family. Like her parents, Wendy had perfect health, striking looks, and high intelligence. She grew up sharing her parents' interests. As John Mink put it, "Discussing issues is a big part of family life—Patsy, Wendy, and me. We're a completely political family, and we enjoy each other's company."

Wendy was twenty-three now. She was at Cornell University, where she was studying politics. All through school, she'd been an outstanding scholar. In time, she would be prepared to teach at a university, if that's what she wanted.

And Wendy could have just about anything she wanted, her parents thought. That was until 1975.

It was then that Patsy received a letter that struck her heart with terror. It was a letter whose history went back to Patsy's pregnancy. At that time, she had gone to a clinic at the University of Chicago. There she was given "vitamins." She learned now that they hadn't been vitamins.

Without being told, she'd been part of an experiment on pregnant women. The "vitamins" were a drug called DES. The experimenters thought DES might prevent miscarriages. Now it had been discovered that it was useless for that purpose. Instead, it could have a number of terrible effects. These included danger of cancer to children born of DES mothers. Grandchildren were at risk of having abnormal brains and diseased organs.

Wendy's parents lost no time in getting her to a medical doctor. No cancer was detected. But as Patsy says, "My daughter has to be examined at least every six months. She will have to live under this threat for the rest of her life." She pauses, shakes her head. "I can't be tough about it. If the danger were to me, I could deal with it. But the danger is to my child."

Besides the anguish and fear, there was anger. "It took almost five years for the University Medical Hospital to notify me. They claimed it was hard to trace the DES women."

But I had been a member of the House of Representatives in the Congress of the United States, with much visibility. Surely it shouldn't have taken them five years to locate me, to give me information on the hazards facing my daughter.

Rep. Mink went public with the information. DES had been used to "treat" other pregnant women throughout the country. Many were still not aware of its effects. Patsy's private agony was the starting point for trying to help others. Years later, she continues to push for education about the effects of DES. Her private pain remains, but her public duty goes on strengthening her "backbone."

If anything could be counted on, it was that Patsy wouldn't keep silent. Perhaps those in control of the hospital knew it. That might account for the fact that it took so long to locate her.

. . .

The last American left Vietnam in April 1975. One year later, the war in Vietnam and Cambodia stumbled to an end.

Patsy's entire career in Congress had been shadowed by the Vietnam War. She had opposed it on many fronts. She'd protested that her country shouldn't be helping Asians to kill Asians. She'd insisted on the public's right to information. She'd defended young men against the draft. She'd been frank in her fury at the waste of billions of dollars for destruction.

She had often been attacked for such "unpatriotic" stands. At the same time, her achievements could not be denied. The *Honolulu Star-Bulletin* had termed her record "brilliant." For example, she'd written and pushed through Congress many bills for education and women's rights. For these and other successes, a lot of voters saw her as a hero. Still others liked her for her independence.

All in all, she'd remained a strong vote-getter. In 1975, she felt ready to put her feet into bigger shoes. She decided to run for the U.S. Senate.

One of Hawaii's two Senators, Hiram Fong, was stepping down. He was a rich businessman, and a Republican. Patsy wasn't the only one to want his seat. Her partner in the House, Spark Matsunaga—like Patsy, a Democrat—also planned to run.

There was no woman in the 100-member Senate at that time. In its entire history, there had only been eleven. Now Patsy was one of six women in the nation making a try for the Senate.

None of the other women had Patsy's experience. Bella Abzug, with two House terms to Patsy's six, came closest. The others had not served in Congress at all. Patsy hoped that victories for women in the Senate would inspire more women to run for both Houses. The time seemed right. Polls showed more and more Americans willing to vote for women at every level.

But changes in the U.S. Senate weren't to happen so soon, after all. All the women running for the Senate were defeated. That included Patsy. She lost the race to Spark Matsunaga.

From the start of the campaign, Patsy had been seen as the underdog. For one thing, the Democratic Party gave its support to Rep. Matsunaga. For another, his campaign fund was twice the size of hers. Also, Matsunaga was a war hero, a veteran of Hawaii's famous 100th Battalion. Finally, in Patsy's words, Matsunaga was a "follower." He could be counted on to stay in the exact middle of Democratic opinion. Patsy, on the other hand, charted her own course. Some didn't like that.

But almost all those things had been true in past elections. And in those, she had been the winner.

Whatever the reasons, this time she had lost. Now it was time to clear out of her Honolulu campaign headquarters. Volunteers pulled down the streamers of orange and blue. Those had been Patsy's campaign colors. She and John took posters from the walls, swept up a last time. Then they locked the door. It was impossible not to feel a little sad—even, a little lost. John took Patsy's hand as they walked to their car.

The next afternoon, she was back at work in the Capitol. On January 3, 1977, when the new Congress was seated, her Washington, D.C. office had been cleared out. By then, her sturdy spirit had bounced back from defeat.

By then, she had a new job, too. In Congress, Patsy

had worked for years on environmental matters. She had become an expert in that field. Now the newly elected President, Jimmy Carter, had asked her to serve as Assistant Secretary for Oceans and Environmental Affairs. It was a highly placed job. Her appointment was seen as a victory for the women's movement.

Unfortunately, the victory did not live long. Patsy found that she had little freedom to make decisions in her new post. She didn't care to keep the job just for the glory of it. After little more than a year, she resigned.

She was soon aboard a plane, heading homeward to Hawaii.

CHAPTER 9

A New Day Dawning

Hammer in hand, John Mink stepped back from the wall. He stared at the picture he'd just put up.

"It doesn't look right, Patsy. Are you sure it was on this wall before?"

Patsy set down a box of teacups. She too stared at the wall. "I don't know. . . ." After a moment, she began to laugh. She sank down on the couch. "I've had all I can *do* of this stuff!"

John smiled. "Agreed," he said. "Let's finish tomorrow."

Patsy looked around the room, sunny in the evening light. She and John were moving back into their house, near Honolulu. They had begun renting it out when Patsy first went to Congress. She'd never gotten used to "having no house" on her trips home.

She felt very happy now. It felt good to be in her own home again. Good to know she could *stay* a while. She didn't need to catch a plane tomorrow, to rush back to Washington. She wouldn't work her usual sixteen-hour day here, either. In Hawaii, the pace of life is a little slower.

Still, Patsy didn't slow down much. At fifty-one, she was bursting with energy. Almost before the last picture was back in place, Patsy was ready to go.

She was ready to go back to her law practice. She soon went back to teaching at the University of Hawaii, too. And before long—she was ready to go back to running for office.

She started close to home. In 1983, she ran for the Honolulu City Council. Old friends and volunteers from past campaigns teased her. "Hey, Patsy!" they said. "Are you wearing your running shoes again?" But they were ready to help.

Patsy won a seat on the council, two terms in a row. She also ran for other offices close to home. In 1986, she tried for Governor of Hawaii. In 1988, she ran for Mayor of Honolulu.

In both these attempts, she was defeated.

Patsy had rarely been defeated in her long political career. Her first defeat had been when Daniel Inouye beat her for a seat in Congress, in 1959. She had taken that set-back hard. She'd said, at that time, "A defeat, after all, is a rejection. One loses the confidence to run again."

Yet she *had* run again. It took courage. But there was more to it than that. Patsy had gone into politics as a way to make a better world. Losing a race didn't change that aim. By the time she lost her 1976 try for the U.S. Senate, she could say, "Life is not based on being an elected politician. Politics is a constant involvement in the day-to-day working of society as a whole, one part of which is government."

She had stayed involved, in Hawaii politics and also in national politics. With dismay, she'd seen social welfare programs she'd worked for in Congress being weakened. President Ronald Reagan, who took office in 1980, didn't believe the federal government should pay for social welfare programs. On the other hand, he urged increases in military spending. Patsy spoke out against his policies. She didn't have to be in Congress to do that.

And then, in 1990, a way opened for her return to Congress.

. . .

It wasn't Patsy's idea, at first. It was John's.

Spark Matsunaga, still serving in the U.S. Senate, died before completing his third term. One of Hawaii's two U.S. House members, Daniel Akaka, was appointed to the vacant Senate seat. A special election was needed, then, to fill Akaka's House seat.

"Patsy," John said, "you must run."

Patsy reached down to scratch an ear of the cat sitting at her feet. She made a face. "Oh, dear."

"No, really. You can't stay out of this," said John. "Of course," he added, "I'll help you."

"You really want to take it on? All over again? There'll be so much to *do*."

But she was halfway there. Her husband's support made the difference. "I would not have done it this second time around without his encouragement," she says today. She jokes about his endless work for her. "He's been in *every* campaign since I *started*. So he's worn out!" But she knows that John Mink's energy is equal to her own.

"When I made the decision to run," she recalls, "it was with a tremendous amount of glee."

Her eyes sparkle.

"And of course, winning made it even greater!"

. . .

More than twenty-five years had passed since the first

time Patsy went to Congress. Her life was somewhat different when she returned in 1991.

This time, only two of the Mink family needed to move to Washington, D.C. By now, Wendy Mink had become a professor, teaching at the University of California in Santa Cruz. John Mink was able to do some of his work away from his Hawaii office. He divides his time between Honolulu and Washington. So the Minks have settled for a small Washington apartment. "It's nothing much, just a place for a cup of coffee," Patsy says.

There is hardly time even for that. "I get home very late every night, past midnight, usually. So, I just pass out from fatigue and get up the next morning—and go to work again."

In her work, she took up old battles and added new ones. No sooner was she in office than she was at odds with the military again. This time, she fought against plans for a military missile site on the Hawaiian island of Kauai.

In her earlier career in Congress, Patsy had regularly worked for the rights and welfare of Native Hawaiians. Since then, a movement by these first people of Hawaii had grown in strength. Patsy continued her efforts for Native Hawaiians upon returning to Congress. She worked for recognition of their fishing rights, and to restore their ancient religious sites. She saw to it that a permanent plan was set up for loans to help them start new businesses.

Less than a year after she returned to Congress, Patsy became involved in a new struggle. This one claimed the attention of the entire country. It arose over the choice of a new justice for the U.S. Supreme Court.

The Republican President, George Bush, was under a lot of pressure to appoint an African-American to the court. To please certain Republicans, however, the President wanted a justice who favored strict limits on the rights of minorities and women. The President's choice was Clarence Thomas, a black federal judge. His views on the rights of women and minorities were what the President wanted. But he'd had only fifteen months' experience as a judge. Quite a few people thought he was not well qualified for the high office of Supreme Court justice.

A nominee for the Supreme Court must be approved by the Senate Judiciary Committee. The committee had some reports that Thomas had sexually harassed women he'd worked with. One of the women was Anita Hill, a black lawyer. She was willing to talk to the committee. But the committee did not call her to testify. When questioned by the FBI, Thomas denied the charges. The Senators planned to vote on appointing him, without further investigation.

But the story leaked out to news magazines. Anita Hill then spoke out publicly, in a TV interview. When that happened, there was a great uproar from the public. In one day, one Senator alone reported 1,000 telephone calls. They came largely from angry women.

The Senator who received the calls, however, wasn't a woman. Very few members of Congress were. At that time, only twenty-nine House members were women, while 406 were men. The Senate had ninety-eight men and two women. All fourteen members of its Judiciary Committee were men.

It seemed clear that the men didn't think the charges against Clarence Thomas were such a big deal. They took it for granted that a man might make sexual remarks to a woman he saw at work. They were puzzled that such behavior might make it hard for the woman to do her job

well. And if the man were her boss, they didn't understand why she might be afraid to report him.

But the women in Congress understood. Few had escaped experiences something like Anita Hill's. And, like
women all over the country, they were furious. Seven
women members of the House decided to march on the
Senate. Rep. Mink was among them. They went in a
group, followed by news reporters. They demanded that
the charges against Clarence Thomas be fully investigated.

Their protest was called the first of its kind. Years before, Patsy had testified against a Supreme Court nominee. The issue then, too, was the unequal treatment of
women. But at that time, Patsy had been the lone member
of Congress to take action. Now, more women in Congress joined the first seven in speaking up.

Finally, the Senators decided to delay their vote. They
held public hearings, carried on TV and radio. Yet the
Senators didn't seem to have learned much about sexual
harassment. It was clear that many of them thought something must be wrong with Anita Hill, rather than Clarence
Thomas. In the hearings, various Senators suggested that
Anita Hill was crazy, a publicity-seeker, a liar, or a sex-
maniac. In the end, too, the Senate approved Clarence
Thomas's appointment.

How different it *might* have been, many women
thought. How different, if even half the Senators had been
women! Many women, and a lot of men, too, thought:
It's time for some big changes.

The changes got underway in the year that followed.
By spring of 1992, 150 women were running for the U.S.
House of Representatives. Some twenty were trying for
the U.S. Senate. A record number of women entered state
and local political contests, too. Women's organizations

were able to give more help to women office seekers than ever in the past. Workers flocked to assist the effort. Funds rolled in, and enthusiasm grew.

At first, most people didn't notice the leap in women's political activity. Even Rep. Mink, who had long hoped that more women would enter politics, didn't clearly see it. Interviewed at the beginning of 1992, she said:

> **The women's movement makes a very small difference in any of the women's elections that I'm aware of in the Congress. I don't think they're a key factor. Women's organizations have a very difficult time! They don't have any *money*!**

A woman's decision to run, she said, ought not to depend on expecting the help of women's groups.

> **It's a personal thing. You either feel you have a mission, or you don't. You can't sit around waiting for help. You have to do it on your own. You have to do your own fund-raising and your own gathering of forces. And then, the frosting on the cake that you've already made is to have the support of the women's organizations.**

Patsy was, of course, describing herself. Her own career didn't owe anything to the women's movement. She didn't point that out, however. Her concern was why there weren't more women in elected offices. The biggest problem, she said, was that so *few* women ran for office. "If more women would run, more would win. It's just a factor of numbers."

The numbers were there, in 1992. The year came to be called the "Year of the Woman." That wasn't only because of women office-seekers, but because of women voters. Millions were angry at the Clarence Thomas appointment. Thomas seemed to be cold to the needs and rights of poor and non-white people. Many feared the effect this would have on Supreme Court decisions. He was also known to oppose abortion rights. Women in huge numbers voted for candidates who supported those rights.

When the elections were over, Congress had a new look and a lot of new voices. The number of women Senators tripled, from two to six. In the House, the number of women almost doubled, going from twenty-nine to forty-eight. Every newly elected woman, Republican and Democrat, supported abortion rights.

Still another big change happened which gave Congress a new look. When Patsy Mink began her career in Congress, she was the first woman of color ever to join that body. There were now fourteen women of color in the House. And for the first time in history, a black woman, Carol Moseley-Braun, became a Senator.

A new day had surely dawned. It was too soon to tell how different the new day would be from the old, as yet.

Patsy Takemoto Mink is no longer the unusual addition to Congress that she once was. Others are taking a path where once she dared to step alone—an Asian-American, and a woman. She is delighted that this is so. Year after year, she has created, and pushed through Congress, projects that encourage girls and women to high achievement. She is herself a model of achievement.

She has reached her goals without leaving her ideals behind. She has never forsaken her passionate struggle for peace and for "simple justice and equality." For Patsy Mink, success in politics cannot be separated from service. She puts it this way:

The key, the only thing that counts is whether a woman is genuinely dedicated to the ideal of doing something that will make a difference to her community and her country. If she has this drive, if she's convinced she can make a contribution, if she's serious and has worked hard and shown the ability to take positions and to stand behind them, to fight for her beliefs, then she cannot fail at an election. I believe this totally.

PATSY T. MINK
(1927–   )

Outline of Life Events

December 6, 1927. Born Paia, Maui, Hawaii. One brother, Eugene. In 1928, family moves to plantation town of Hamakuapoko, Maui.

Dec. 7, 1941–June 1944. Pearl Harbor bombed. Ill treatment of Japanese-Americans follows, awakening her to racism, injustice. Student-body president, class valedictorian at Maui High School. Plans to become medical doctor.

1944–46. University of Hawaii, Honolulu, at age sixteen. Two years later, to Wilson College, Chambersburg, Pennsylvania. January 1947, transfers to University of Nebraska, Lincoln. Protests racial discrimination in student housing. Others join the protest, leading to desegregation of student quarters.

1947–48. Returns to Honolulu. Graduates University of Hawaii, with B.A. in zoology and chemistry. Applies to more than a dozen medical schools and is turned down by all.

1949–51. Attends University of Chicago School of Law. Marries John Mink, graduate student in geology. Receives law degree, but finds no work in Chicago law firms.

1952. Birth of daughter, Gwendolyn. Returns to Honolulu with husband and child.

1953. Takes bar exam and becomes first woman of Japanese ancestry admitted to Hawaii bar. Does not succeed in search for Honolulu law firm job. Opens her own law office.

1953–62. Joins movement for reform of Hawaii's Democratic Party. Organizes in Hawaii for Young Democrats of America and is elected its national vice-president. In **1956,** becomes first Nisei woman elected to Hawaii's territorial legislature. Elected to senate, **1958.** Works for equal pay for women and educational reform. **March 12, 1959,** Hawaii admitted to U.S. as fiftieth state. Runs for U.S. Congress, but defeated in primary by Daniel Inouye. Continues law practice and lecturing at University of Hawaii.

1962–64. Wins senate seat in Hawaii state legislature. In **1964,** tries again for U.S. House, and wins. Is first woman of color elected to Congress.

1965–77. Serves unbroken twelve years in U.S. House. Obtains appointment to the Education and Labor Committee. Works tirelessly on many issues, including: halting nuclear weapons testing, ending the Vietnam War, amnesty for evaders of military draft; support of civil rights and liberties, busing, school lunch programs, bilingual education, education for handicapped persons, family assistance programs, federal funding of daycare centers, federal aid for abortions, conservation, environmental protection. **1970,** first witness and only member of Congress to testify against nominee for Supreme Court Associate Justice G. Harrold Carswell, on grounds of his insensitivity to women's rights. Sets off chain reaction that defeats the nomination. Writes and sponsors Women's Educational Equity Act (signed into law, **1974**), providing for increase in women's educational and job opportunities.

1975. Learns that during her pregnancy she was part of a medical experiment in which women were given the drug DES, later proved harmful to children of such women. Speaks out strongly to inform and warn DES women.

1976. Makes bid for seat of retiring Hawaii Senator Hiram Fong. Is defeated in Democratic primary, halting her Congressional career.

1977. Appointed by President Jimmy Carter to State Department position of Assistant Secretary for Oceans and International Environmental and Scientific Affairs. Resigns, **1978.**

1983–87. Elected to two terms, Honolulu City Council.

1986. Runs for governor of Hawaii. Finishes third, in Democratic primary.

1988. Loses in primary bid for Honolulu mayoralty.

1990–2. Urged by John Mink, enters and wins special election for U.S. House seat. Back in Congress, takes same positions as before, including opposition to militarism, strong support for education, environmental protection, civil rights. Is one of the first group of women in Congress to attack the Senate for neglecting sexual harassment charges against Clarence Thomas, nominee for Supreme Court Associate Justice.

1992. Re-elected to the U.S. House of Representatives.

Glossary

Amendment: A change or addition to the Constitution.

Bill: A proposal for a law, written down, to present to a legislature, but not yet passed and made law.

Boycott: A refusal to buy certain goods, as a protest.

Buddhist: A person whose faith is Buddhism, a religion followed mostly in Asia, but also in other parts of the world.

Campaign: (1) A contest for public office by rival political candidates. (2) An organized attempt to bring about a change in laws or policies.

Civil disobedience: Peaceful, deliberate breaking of a law, done openly, to try to call attention to an injustice. Its purpose may be: to get a change in a policy; to get a law changed; to get a law enforced; to get a new law. Persons doing the action do not try to escape arrest for their law-breaking.

Civil rights movement: The struggle of African-Americans to gain equal rights, beginning with the time after slavery. In modern times, it means the 1950s-1960s movement led by Dr. Martin Luther King, Jr.

Communist: A system of government in which a single political party makes all the important decisions and controls the work that needs to be done, as well as what is produced by that work. For many years, from about 1945 to about 1989, the United States struggled with Communist countries for world power. *Communist* also means a member of a Communist party.

Congress: See *legislature*, below.

Constitution: A written plan of government. The U.S. Constitution describes the powers of the federal government.

Convention: A meeting called by an organized group, to discuss and act upon matters of interest to the group.

Depression; Great Depression: A time, starting in 1929 and lasting through most of the 1930s, when businesses failed and millions of people were unemployed.

Discrimination: Treatment in favor of, or against, a person because of the group he or she belongs to, such as a racial group.

Feminism: Support of rights for women equal to those of men.

Feminist: A person who believes in equal rights for women.

Haole: Hawaiian word for white person.

Hindu: A person who practices Hinduism, the main religion of India.

Impeach: The legal process of accusing a public official of wrongdoing.

Inauguration: Ceremony in which the President or other high government official takes the oath of office.

Legislator: A member of a legislature; a lawmaker.

Legislature: The branch of government that makes laws. In the United States, *Congress* is the legislature of the federal government. It is made up of the House of Representatives and the Senate. Each state has two Senators and is represented in the House according to the size of its population. Each state and *territory* also has a legislature.

Lobby: An effort to convince public officials to support the policies favored by a particular group.

Lobbyist: A person who tries to influence public officials to support the policies favored by a particular group.

Muslim: A person who follows the religious beliefs of Islam. The founder of the religion was the prophet Muhammad.

Nazi party; Nazis: National Socialist German Workers Party. It seized and held power in Germany (1933-1945) under the dictator Adolph Hitler. It promoted racism and the belief that the German people were superior to all others.

Nazism: The ideas or methods of the Nazis.

Pacifism: Opposition to war and organized violence of any kind.

Pacifist: A person who believes in pacifism.

Petition: A written request made to a government official or a group of officials, signed by a number of people.

Picket: A person who demonstrates, often with a sign, against something she or he believes is unfair.

Plank: A part of the platform of a political party. See *platform*, next.

Platform: A statement of the positions taken by a political party on some of the issues of the day.

Primary election: An election in which voters of each political party choose their candidates for public offices. The winners then run against each other in the next election.

Reform: To improve something that seems wrong or unfair.

Reformer: A person who works for reform.

Resolution: An official statement by a legislature, giving its opinion, or what it aims to do, about an issue.

Saree (also, *sari*): A type of garment worn by many women in India; it is a long piece of cloth wrapped around the body, with one end draped over the shoulder or head.

Sexism: Discrimination based on a person's sex (most often directed at women), as in limits on job opportunities.

Sexist: Views and behavior that support sexism. A person with such views and behavior.

Shinto: The main religion of Japan.

Socialist: A system in which government or the people as a whole own and control business and all other important economic parts of society. *Socialist* also means a member of a Socialist party.

Suffrage: The right to vote. Also, shorthand for women's right to vote during the years of struggle for woman suffrage.

Suffragist: A woman working for women's right to vote.

Territory: An area of the U.S. not admitted as a state but having its own legislature, with a governor appointed by the President.

Veto: The power to kill a bill passed by Congress.

Woman suffrage: The right of women to vote.

Bill Hanson

SUE DAVIDSON is the author of *Getting the Real Story: Nellie Bly and Ida B. Wells*, the first title in the "Women Who Dared" series. She is the co-author of *You Can Be Free: An Easy-To-Read Handbook for Abused Women* (Seal, 1989), and the co-editor of *A Needle, A Bobbin, A Strike: Women Needleworkers in America* (Temple University Press, 1984) and of *The Maimie Papers* (The Feminist Press, 1977).

Originally from Texas, where she worked on the editorial staff of the *Galveston Daily News*, Davidson makes her home in Seattle, Washington. She has been a participant in many movements for peace and social justice. Her longest associations have been with the War Resisters League and the American Civil Liberties Union. She is a member of PEN.

Selected Titles from Seal Press

GETTING THE REAL STORY: *Nellie Bly and Ida B. Wells* by Sue Davidson. $8.95, 1-878067-16-8. The first book in the **Women Who Dared Series** is filled with exciting information on the lives of two courageous women who were journalists in the 1860s. Nellie Bly's "behind-the-scenes" stories led to social reforms. Ida B. Wells was an African-American activist whose writings sparked the formation of many organizations dedicated to civil rights and equality.

NO MORE SECRETS by Nina Weinstein. $8.95, 1-878067-00-1. A beautifully written and sensitive novel for young adults and survivors of sexual abuse of all ages, this coming-of-age story tells of sixteen-year-old Mandy's recovery from a childhood rape. Winner of the American Library Association Award for Best Book for Young Adults.

YOU CAN BE FREE: *An Easy-To-Read Handbook for Abused Women* by Ginny NiCarthy and Sue Davidson. $8.95, 0-931188-68-7. A simplified version of *Getting Free,* the most important book of the domestic violence movement.

GETTING FREE: *You Can End Abuse and Take Back Your Life* by Ginny NiCarthy. $12.95, 0-931188-37-7. Written for women who are being physically battered or emotionally abused in their relationships, *Getting Free* offers support, practical help and inspiration.

IN LOVE AND IN DANGER: *A Teen's Guide to Breaking Free of Abusive Relationships* by Barrie Levy. $8.95, 1-878067-26-5. An important, straightforward book for teens caught in abusive dating relations. Includes first-hand stories from teenagers and practical advice on how to recognize and end abuse.

HARD-HATTED WOMEN: *Stories of Struggle and Success in the Trades* edited by Molly Martin. $12.95, 0-931188-66-0. Vivid and inspiring accounts of life on the job by twenty-six tradeswomen.

SHE'S A REBEL: *The History of Women in Rock & Roll* by Gillian G. Gaar. $16.95, 1-878067-08-7. Packed with interviews, facts and personal anecdotes from women performers, writers and producers, *She's A Rebel* tells the fascinating story of the women who have shaped rock and pop music for the last four decades.

SEAL PRESS, founded in 1976 to provide a forum for women writers and feminist issues, has many other books of fiction and non-fiction, including books on health and self-help, sports and outdoors, mysteries and non-fiction anthologies. You can order the books listed above by writing to 3131 Western Avenue, Suite 410, Seattle, Washington 98121 (please add 15% of the book total for shipping and handling). Write to us for a free catalog.